D0502976

# A CIVIL
# TONGUE

*Also by Edwin Newman*

Strictly Speaking:
Will America Be the Death of English?

# A CIVIL TONGUE

BY

## EDWIN NEWMAN

THE BOBBS-MERRILL COMPANY, INC.
*Indianapolis/New York*

Copyright © 1975, 1976 by Edwin H. Newman
All rights reserved, including the right of reproduction
in whole or in part in any form
Published by the Bobbs-Merrill Company, Inc.
Indianapolis / New York
Designed by Jacques Chazaud
Manufactured in the United States of America
Third Printing—1976

**Library of Congress Cataloging in Publication Data**

Newman, Edwin.
  A civil tongue.

  1.  English language in the United States.  2.  Sociolinguistics.  3.  United  States—Social  life  and
customs.  I.  Title.
PE2808.N39        301.2′1        76–11607
ISBN  0–672–52267–5

For
my wife
and
daughter

# Contents

# Acknowledgments

I owe thanks not only to my wife and daughter, to whom this book is dedicated, but to Jeannette Hopkins, who was the editor; Carol Bok, who did the research; and Mary Heathcote, the copy editor; and to NBC News. Much of what I have written is based on information and experience that I have gained as an NBC correspondent.

I am grateful to *Esquire* and *Change* magazines for permission to use, in altered form, material that first appeared in their pages.

# After I,
# the Deluge

W hen I was a lad, I did not serve a term as office boy to an attorney's firm. It was one of a number of omissions. I did, however, work for a while as a file clerk in a credit agency. Since I was sixteen years old at the time and had been graduated from high school, I knew a great deal and had opinions on a variety of subjects that I thought anyone else in the office would consider it a privilege to hear. I also thought that I discerned flaws in the way the office was run. One fine day I was advised to keep a civil tongue in my head. That meant "Be respectful to your elders," or less gently interpreted, "Shut up." Although I did not know the word at the time (nobody did), I prioritized my interests, even as Jimmy Carter many years later suggested that the Democrats prioritize their platform. Having a job was more highly prioritized than not having a job. Shut up I did.

I now take a civil tongue to mean much more than that. Mere politeness is part of it, though the temptation to place mere before politeness ought to be resisted. The alternative to a code of conduct is, if not chaos, certainly confusion and embarrassment, and language is conduct. Not that I am arguing for freezing the language. I would hate to take American English out of a cryogenic compartment in a hundred years and find, after the ice is chipped away and the language has thawed, that it sounds as it does now. I think I would put it back in.

How *does* it sound now? It does not sound civil.

"It's not nice to be a child molester," says a Connecticut penologist, "but if you're a junkie, you can find all kinds of peer support." That is the kind of support everybody wants. When I walk into NBC News in the morning and see another correspondent, I say, "Good morning, peer." "Peer greetings to you," the other is likely, in peer-shaped tones, to reply.

A Puerto Rican scholar writes, "Our children currently have no viable role models to emulate." Heroes they would have been called not long ago. And heroines. But that is too straightforward:

"Father, I cannot tell a lie. With my little hatchet, I chopped down the cherry tree."

"I'm proud of you, George. I was saying to your mother only last week that one day our son will be a role model for generations of Americans yet unborn."

A New York specialty shop advertises items "for all the giftees on your June list." I hope it spreads to Scotland:

"Wha hae ye there, lass?"

"Tis a wee giftie for the giftee."

"Aye, would some power the giftee gie us . . ."

The Mayor of New York, Abraham Beame, emits a Bicentennial comment: "Where else but in an American democracy could a boy of the Lower East Side, born in London to parents fleeing Russian discrimination, grow up to be mayor of a panethnic city?" The merry, merry pipes of pan-ethnicity, and the usual tune.

Scientists investigating spontaneous glucagon secretion in the immediate postnatal period study groups of infants cross-sectionally and longitudinally. Cross-sectionally should not alarm anyone: it means at the same age. Longitudinally means as they grow older. A man is put in jail in Dubuque, Iowa. It isn't called the jail any longer; it's the law enforcement center. Time is served there longitudinally. When the soil-collecting scoop on Viking I on Mars fails to function, an anomaly team goes to work to set it right. No hits, no runs, no anomalies.

Washington churns out its usual nonsense. The chief of the United States Capitol Police posts a notice: "Vehicles will be parked chronologically as they enter the lot" (1975 models in this corner and 1973 models over there). The Undersecretary of the Treasury, Edwin H. Yeo III, is asked about additional loans to New York City: "If we find the reasonable probability of repayment is slipping away from us, then we'll have to respond in terms of extension of future credit." If they don't pay what they owe, we won't lend them any more. President Ford returns from a trip to China, Indonesia, and the Philippines in December 1975 and enunciates a Pacific Doctrine. It is never heard of again, but many Presidents believe that the right to enunciate a doctrine goes with the office. United Press International quotes an assistant to Vice President Rockefeller: "Ford not only let the Rockefeller juggernaut come down from New York, but has us in his stable now." The juggernaut, which had to lower its head to get in, is given the stall next to the Ford bandwagon. Both are let out occasionally to roll a bit, but not far.

The sports world makes its contribution. Don Rock, vice president of the National Hockey League, speaks disapprovingly of players who fester a grudge. The grudge may burst and spray those in range with rancor. A weather broadcaster in Marlboro, Massachusetts, calls small storms stormettes. Massachusetts come from a small Massachus. In Kansas City, Missouri, television viewers are told about "the heavy storm system that performed over our area last night." Music by Rossini. An airline stewardess urges her passengers to "have a nice day in Cincinnati or wherever your final destination may be taking you," and an investment company writes: "We have exceptional game plan capabilities together with strict concerns for programming successful situations." My final destination is taking me far away from game plans, capabilities, programming, and situations, there to have a nice day. A pro-

fessor, Sam Schoenbaum of Northwestern, explains on ABC television why William Shakespeare was so eminent a playwright:
"He had a tremendous commitment to his own medium, the
stage." All the world's a medium, but the professor appears to
believe that Shakespeare could have left the theater for television
or Hollywood.

That is how the language sounds now. A civil tongue, on the
other hand, means to me a language that is not bogged down in
jargon, not puffed up with false dignity, not studded with trick
phrases that have lost their meaning. It is not falsely exciting, is
not patronizing, does not conceal the smallness and triteness of
ideas by clothing them in language ever more grandiose, does not
seek out increasingly complicated constructions, does not weigh
us down with the gelatinous verbiage of Washington and the
social sciences. It treats errors in spelling and usage with a decent
tolerance but does not take them lightly. It does not consider
"We're there because that's where it's at" the height of cleverness.
It is not merely a stream of sound that disk jockeys produce, in
which what is said does not matter so long as it is said without
pause. It is direct, specific, concrete, vigorous, colorful, subtle,
and imaginative when it should be, and as lucid and eloquent as
we are able to make it. It is something to revel in and enjoy.

Unfortunately, it is also only a dream, for an ironic thing
is happening in the United States. As we demand more and more
personal openness from those in public life—unwisely, it seems to
me—our language becomes more and more covered, obscure,
turgid, ponderous, and overblown. The candor expected of public
officials about their health, their money, their private lives, or
what used to be thought of as their private lives, is offset in public
matters by language that conceals more than it tells, and often
conceals the fact that there is little or nothing worth telling.

We increasingly expect of those holding office an accounting
of their financial holdings and their health. There are some who
want a panel of psychiatrists to examine all who seek high office,
to determine whether they can be trusted with public affairs and
with their private ones. The way things are going, there will

probably be a demand that those in public life give assurances that their sexual undertakings leave them without anxiety and ready to turn to affairs of state without lurid dreams that trouble their sleep. This demand will be strengthened by its having been reported that by the time Watergate reached its denouement, Richard and Pat Nixon had not slept together in fourteen years. During the furor over the liaison between Wayne Hays, chairman of the House Administration Committee, and Elizabeth Ray, a committee employee and Hays's mistress-turned-novelist, the Speaker of the House, Carl Albert, dealing with reports of orgies in his office, felt it necessary to say that he was sixty-eight and had not slept with a woman all year. (It was early June.)

I would be willing to get along with less information about this or that officeholder's tax return or bedroom activities if I could get him or her to speak more clearly about matters of public policy. When the press resolved to be thrilled by Henry Kissinger's bachelor exploits, I was less interested in knowing who his dinner companions were than in knowing what diplomatic agreements he was making and what obligations he was taking on for the United States. Early in the 1976 campaign the White House objected to press and television pictures of President Ford falling down while skiing. The obvious response is that the White House should not announce "photo opportunities" of the President skiing. A few months later it ruled out photo opportunities when he boarded a helicopter on the White House lawn because of unseemly publicity over the times he had bumped his head on earlier occasions. I must add, however, that I did not understand why there should have been any interest in the pictures. Skiers do fall down, just as tall men sometimes bump their heads on low airplane doorways. I have bumped my head, and my height—I stand seventy-three and a half inches nearer the stars—is not exceptional. It says nothing about my prowess as a news commentator. By the same token, Ford could be the greatest skier alive and that would have nothing to do with his ability to be President. When Betty Ford was asked what her reaction would be if her daughter had an affair, she replied that she would not be surprised.

I thought the proper reply was "None of your business." I certainly regarded it as none of mine.

It is easy to understand the insistence that public men and women tell all, especially after Vietnam, Watergate, the resignation of a President and a Vice President, and various financial scandals and sexual escapades. What we ought to be demanding is that our leaders speak better English, so that we know what they are talking about and, incidentally, so that *they* do. The disclosure of such information as number of shares held, money in the bank, condition of kidneys, creates the impression that something is being done to protect us. For the most part it is an illusion. There is little salvation to be found in more psychiatry and less privacy. Some safety does lie in more sensible public attitudes, especially toward the public relations and advertising techniques now widely used by politicians. It lies in understanding that there can be many sources of leadership in the country, not the White House alone. It lies also in independent reporting by those of us in the news business, in greater skepticism on the part of the public, and in an unremitting puncturing of the overblown. In all of this, language is crucial. Let us go forward into a charismaless future.

A woman in Goshen, Indiana, told me recently that her daughter-in-law, for whom English is a second language, was sitting on the floor one day in despair, surrounded by housekeeping items to be kept, put in the attic, or given away. "So many junk," she said.

English, thanks to many for whom it is the first language, is in the same beleaguered position, hopelessly burdened by so many junk, which should not be kept, or put in the attic, or given away, but thrown away. If you drink, exclude vehicle use, says the California Highway Patrol. That should be thrown away. So should "In order to improve security, we request that, effective immediately, no employees use the above subject doors for ingress and egress to the building." The New York corporation that perpetrated that made ingress and egress sound as portentous as yin and yang. It should be egress from, and the company could have said entering and leaving. Or simply, Don't open these doors.

There are few other things to do with doors, even of the subject kind.* A young man writes to a Maine newspaper about an older man who "became an experiencing person in my life, lending an aura to my developing personality of absolute rapport and communicatory relevance." Evidently the older man was sympathetic and understanding. A civil tongue would have said so.

The Asbury Park, New Jersey, *Press* runs a story from Washington about a restaurant where important people go and where "dinner table banter transubstantiates into lunch." A small miracle, and without benefit of clergy. *Time* magazine reports Henry Kissinger's appearing "perceptibly relaxed." When Kissinger appears imperceptibly relaxed, reporters cluster around knowing that something is brewing. The *New York Times* writes an editorial: "Given the political balance in Congress, it is specifically up to the Democratic leadership in both houses to take initiatives that have so far been unimpressive." Why the *Times* wants the Democrats to recommend again courses already found wanting I am unable to figure out. The *Times* reports on a trial from North Haverhill, New Hampshire: "The Eames brothers contended that their mother, and not them, manages the theatre." Them were acquitted.

A Winston-Salem, North Carolina, budget proposal calls for money for "effective confinement and extinguishment of unwanted and destructive fires." Firemen unable to achieve distinguishment between unwanted and destructive fires and the wanted and constructive kind probably are destined to suffer languishment in the lower grades. Those of us devoted to a civil tongue suffer anguishment. The Winston-Salem budget also proposes "schedule adherence with emphasis on hitting checkpoints within the targeted time." That's making the buses run on schedule. It calls for "human interment space." Cemeteries.

When I entered the news business thirty-five years ago, I thought that I had taken an oath to preserve, protect, and defend the English language, as a President swears that he will preserve,

* Another possibility: Exclude door use.

protect, and defend the Constitution. I have tried to honor the oath, as have many others, in and out of news, but now it seems to me that American English, vigorous, adaptable, and resourceful, a treasure trove of wit, charm, and inspiration, may soon be lowered into a language interment space with a marker erected bearing the words Actuarially Matured. The interment unit diggers are all about us.

Late in 1974 the Secretary of Commerce, Frederick Dent, said that the rate of inflation in the second quarter of the year was 9.6 per cent, and this "validated the essentiality of President Ford's struggle to cut the inflation rate." A civil tongue would have said justified, but that would have cost Dent three words and nine syllables and, in the way of Washington, which would never say satellite photography when it could say technical overhead reconnaissance, commensurate self-respect. In March 1975, FBI agents and local policemen broke into an apartment in Alexandria, Virginia, because of a tip that Patricia Hearst was there. Later, Michael Morrow, assistant special agent in charge of the Aiexandria FBI office, explained that the young woman who lived there would not open the door and "the only reason entry was forced was because of the totality of the situation." Patricia Hearst was not in the apartment, and the FBI stubbed its totality. It should have bitten its uncivil tongue.

A reporter asks Louise Lasser, of the television serial "Mary Hartman, Mary Hartman," what she knows about the boredom of being a housewife. "I don't know anything about the externalism of being in the kitchen," Miss Lasser replies, "but I certainly know about ennui." When I hear words like externalism, I also know about ennui.

The Supervisor of Reading in the schools of Ridgewood, New Jersey, asks parents to provide readiness experiences for their preschool children by encouraging them to reaffirm their perceptions on a tactile level. Parents are to model behavior that characterizes their values. They are never to model oral fragments, but they are to noun. Modeling oral fragments could mean posing for advertisements for chipped teeth, but doesn't. An oral fragment comes into being when you say, "Huh?" or "Wow!" You noun when you identify an object unknown to the child. In Ridgewood, New Jersey, you might say, "This is a supervisor of reading." Wow!

Nelson Rockefeller, when asked whether he would be nominated at the 1976 Republican convention, forswore the oral fragment. "I cannot conceive of any scenario in which that could eventuate," he said. Won't things improve when the younger generation of politicians takes over? No. Edmund Brown, Jr., asked whether his 1976 candidacy was really aimed at 1980, replied, "My equation is sufficiently complex to admit of various outcomes." Declining to ride to a money-raising dinner in a chauffeur-driven Mercedes, he explained, "I cannot relate to that material possessory consciousness," and used an unwashed Ford instead. Conspicuous inconspicuous consumption.

There are risks in writing a book in which you find fault with the language of others. It admits of various outcomes. On January 1, 1975, two months after the publication of *Strictly Speaking,* my first book on English, Meb Bolin, of Portales, New Mexico, wished me a Happy New Year and added, "May you survive the precarious position in which you have been placed by your book." It was precarious. I was obliged to agree with Helen M. Leonard, of Eau Claire, Wisconsin, that the phrase "as a matter of fact" was tattered, vacuous, redundant, and pompous, and that I should not have used it when interviewed by Bob Cromie on "Book Beat"; with Marjorie Driver, of Coon Rapids, Minnesota, that I said "It seems to me" too often on the Merv Griffin show; with Mary R. Livingstone, of Winchester, Massachusetts, that "quite a few," which I said on the "Today" show, means nothing; with Stephen C. Adamson, of Stoughton, Massachusetts, that if I said "I myself" on the Merv Griffin show, it must have been for emphasis but that "I" would have been sufficient. I acknowledged to Charles W. Laue, of Atmore, Alabama, that athletes' salaries cannot be infinitely larger than they used to be; to Bernadette Ellis, of East Troy, Wisconsin, that although I said "I don't think . . ." on the Phil Donahue show, I do think and should not deny it; and to

Esther Lafair, of the Center for Studies in Criminology and Criminal Law at the University of Pennsylvania, that in congeries the accent falls on the second syllable, not the first. To the brave belong Lafair, but I had been foolhardy.

In September 1975, I went to Tokyo to interview Emperor Hirohito before his visit to the United States, the first interview the Emperor had ever granted. Discussing it on the "Today" show, I wanted to say that everyone present had been behind a screen except the camera crews and me. I started to say it, but the sentence grew longer, with embellishments being dropped in, and by the end I could not remember how it had begun. Should it be I or me? I went for the fake elegance. After I, the deluge. My equation admitted of a form letter acknowledging error.

There could also have been a form letter *to* me about the title of my book. The Columbia, South Carolina, *State* made it *Strickly Speaking,* though on a best-seller list, which softened the blow. It was also *Strickly Speaking* at the Carnegie Public Library in Rock Springs, Wyoming; in an advertisement by Waldenbooks in the Newark, New Jersey, *Star-Ledger;* in the *Washington Post;* and at the Cecil County Library in Elkton, Maryland, a branch of the New York Public Library, the Minneapolis Public Library, the library in Townshend, Vermont, and the Thomas Jefferson Library System of Jefferson City, Missouri. A Jefferson City woman who asked for the book wrote to me that perhaps she had not spoken distinkly. The publisher of the book, Bobbs-Merrill, occasionally made it *Stricktly Speaking,* which showed a nice impartiality. Charles E. Lyght, a physician in Oklawaha, Florida, and editor-in-chief of the *Journal of the American Geriatrics Society,* ordered the book from a shop in Ocala and in return was promised *Strickley Speaking.* "Good old Strickley," Dr. Lyght wrote to me, "I remember him well."

I consoled myself that the misspellings merely proved the point I had been making. I was more troubled when a company librarian in Omaha, Beatrice Langfeld, wrote that when she asked the public library there how to classify the book, she was told under culture and cultural process, a subhead of sociology. Jane

Wyville, of Yuba City, California, told me that it was classified there under sociolinguistics. It is said that China simply absorbs its invaders. I do not want to be absorbed into sociology, still less a subhead of it. Sociologists are people who pretend to advance the cause of knowledge by calling a family a microcluster of structured role expectations or a bounded plurality of role-playing individuals. Among sociologists, a civil tongue is all but unknown.

A civil tongue should not pretend to command foreign languages that it doesn't. In *Strictly Speaking* a Latin phrase had Nehercule for Mehercule and ea for et. "Lapsūs typographici," Elizabeth Cummings, a Latin teacher in Harrisburg, Pennsylvania, graciously suggested. But as lapsūs go, typographici they were not. My daughter, who studied Latin, which I did not, and who received half the book's dedication, was less indulgent. She asked why I had not consulted her. She knew what kind of lapsūs they were. A librarian in Milton, Massachusetts, E. B. Pile, suggested that when I made certain British heraldic officers Poursuivants of Arms in Ordinary—they are Pursuivants—it was either a typo or a test of the alertness of my readers. I could have replied that poursuivants were British court functionaries who followed royalty around with teapots at the ready and that these matters were in the lapsūs of the gods. Instead, I took the blame myself. Quis custodiet ipsos custodes? Mrs. Pile had wanted to know. It was the sort of question to which, in the early days of television news, we used to respond, "I'm glad you asked me that" (Peropportune hoc rogasti), and then sign off (et tum audientibus valedicas).

Deane W. Malott, president emeritus of Cornell University, reprimanded me about "Boola Boola," the Yale fight song. I had written that boola boola was an adaptation of the Hawaiian hoola boola. "This," Dr. Malott said, in a sentence that was a role model of its kind, "is not correct." Hoola in Hawaii is hula, and boola does not exist because there is no "b" in the Hawaiian alphabet. My information on "Boola Boola" had come from Yale University. Quis custodiet ipsos custodes? Peropportune hoc rogasti. Lux et veritas.

Others in the audientibus were not so gentle. To the question asked by the subtitle of *Strictly Speaking,* Will America Be the Death of English? a reader in Huntington, Pennsylvania, unbidden, answered, "Yes," and predicted that I would be in at the kill. "As I read the book," she wrote, "I hastily jotted down at least 201 errors either in misuse of the introductory And/But when a subordinate conjunction should have been used or in incorrect punctuation." Frank Chesley of the *Seattle Post-Intelligencer* said that I used too many parenthetical expressions, and Florence Way, a retired teacher of English of Los Altos, California (California proved to be full of watchdogs of the language, watching me), complained that I relied too heavily on semicolons. She singled out a sentence with forty-four of them. I had thought it a brilliantly constructed apotheosis of the semicolon. David G. Lynch, of Cincinnati, said that he had read two paragraphs on page 157 over and over without finding a sequitur. It's a matter of knowing where to look. Ask the sequitary.

I wrote that President Kennedy delivered a speech in embarrassed silence. Herman Jervis, of New York, wished that more politicians would follow that course. Linda Wechsler, of Granada Hills, California, suggested that I follow my own advice and eschew more words than are needed. I had written, "No other politician will put in an appearance." Mrs. Wechsler recommended "No politician will appear." I replied in embarrassed silence.

I received gratefully a letter from Mrs. Robert O. Wright, in Peoria, Illinois, who liked the book and was afraid to say more. Miriam Nelson Brown, of Sayville, New York, gave herself a B-minus for her letter and added, "I have had this graded to save you the trouble." Jane Robison, a professor of English in South Carolina, suggested that any errors in the book probably had been planted there by me for the pleasure of teachers like her, an idea that escaped my professors years before. It reminded me of the time I interviewed the actor Dustin Hoffman in a glassed-in restaurant. As word spread of what was happening, young women gathered outside to stare in. Hoffman got up and went to the window. "Where were you when I needed you?" he shouted.

Those who complain about the misuse of English are widely

regarded as quaint and to be pointed out to tourists. Yet we are not such an exotic growth. After *Strictly Speaking* was published, I heard, as might have been expected, from teachers of English and of Latin, and from authors and editors, but also from judges, lawyers, doctors, members of Congress and of state legislatures; from employees of Congress, the CIA, NASA, the Federal Communications Commission, and a variety of other federal, state, city and county agencies; from foundation executives, retired people—some of them in old soldiers' homes—housewives, businessmen, airline pilots, newspeople, brokers, secretaries and accountants. There was a letter from Lois DeBakey, professor of scientific communications, Baylor College of Medicine, Houston, Texas, who tries to dissuade physicians from writing "There were four deaths, only one of which lived more than two months," and to persuade them to say swallowing instead of deglutination. A clergyman, Monsignor Charles J. Plauché, of Saint Francis Cabrini Church in New Orleans, wrote to say that he thought his days as a pastor were numbered. Unless the trend in language was reversed, he expected to become Coordinator of the Faith Community Dimension. Monsignor Plauché is probably right. Community is rampant, and I am surprised not to have been placed in the media community dimension. Particularly endearing are references to the intelligence community. It is as though the head of the CIA raps on the door of the director of Naval Intelligence to ask what sort of day he had and borrow a cup of sugar.

Letters cheering me on in the struggle for the language* have come from people in their nineties and from students, among the latter one in the ninth grade who spotted a mistake in an article about me in *People* magazine. So age is not a factor in concern for the language. Nor is it a concern only to the highly educated, or the effete Northeast, or to city folk. I have heard from Palouse, Washington; Decatur, Georgia; Morristown, Tennessee; Nakomis, Florida; Potsdam, New York; Jamestown, California; Brunswick, Maine; LaPorte, Texas; DePere, Wisconsin; Health Springs, South

---

* Though not validating its essentiality.

Carolina; Wallingford, Pennsylvania; Rocky Mount, North Carolina; Rocky River, Ohio; Fort Branch, Indiana; Kemenick,
Washington; and Alpena, South Dakota. Some of the most impas-
sioned letters have come from people who were not born in the
United States, who worked hard to learn English and to use it well,
and who were puzzled and pained by the language's decline.
Others came from Canada, Australia, and Britain, and some from
readers with APO and FPO addresses whose precise whereabouts
could not be known. Hundreds volunteered material for a second
book. Much of that material I have used. *A Civil Tongue* is my
response.

Such support is immensely gratifying to an author, but I
understand that it came to me because I was, so to speak, standing
proxy for the English language. Some of my readers wrote to
newspaper, magazine, radio, and television editors calling their
attention to infelicities and asking, "What would Edwin Newman
think?" The editors appeared not to consider this a pressing
question.

I have been, as a consequence of all this, invited to join the
Queen's English Society, which was formed in 1972 by some
people in Britain who "felt very concerned about the decline of
literacy since the War." The society offers its letterheads to members "to give weight to their communications with the press or
BBC." I wish the Queen's English Society well, but I did not join
it and I would not join a comparable organization here. There is
no office of state to name it for, and a very good thing that is.
The assertion of authority in these matters rarely succeeds. Besides, if American English is burdened with so many junk, the
United States Government is the burdener-in-chief, with a large
part of the gross national product devoted to the purpose. In this,
policy is bipartisan, all branches join in, and checks and balances
and the separation of powers are ignored. Beyond that, societies,
committees, and the like are almost invariably a source of deplor-
able English themselves. If American English is to be saved, it
will, in my view, have to be saved by individuals, or by small
guerrilla groups that refuse to accept nonsense, send back unclear

and pompous letters with a request for a translation, and insist that organizations they are part of speak plainly. This cannot be done on orders from above. It requires rebelliousness, buccaneering, and humor, qualities that organizations are short of.

Fortunately, practitioners of a civil tongue do exist. A reporter asked the head of the AFL-CIO, George Meany, for his analysis of the elections of November 1974. What was the people's mandate? Said Meany: "I don't believe in this mandate stuff. A guy runs for office and gets elected. All of a sudden he's got a mandate. Two less votes and he's nothing." A good mandate is hard to find.

A more cautiously phrased example of the civil tongue in action came from William Bateman, executive vice president of the Chase Manhattan Bank. When asked about the difficulties faced by real estate investment trusts, he said, "We're not anxious to see anything with the name Chase Manhattan in bankruptcy anywhere." Bateman should have said eager, not anxious, but the understatement was pleasant.

A civil tongue knows when to remain silent. Over the years, heads of state and heads of government have convinced themselves that their countries will lose prestige, and so will they, if they do not claim the right to deliver tedious speeches whenever possible. At the United Nations the consequence is that everybody assures everybody else of the need for peace and justice and progress, and archives result. In September 1974, Prime Minister Pierre Trudeau of Canada decided not to speak because he had nothing sufficiently important to say. Trudeau's gesture was little noticed. It should have made him immortal.

As little noticed was a gesture two months earlier by Norris Cotton. On July 3, 1974, President Nixon spoke in Caribou, Maine, about the visit he had just made to the Soviet Union. A reporter asked Cotton, then a Republican Senator from New Hampshire, for his reaction. "I cannot comment directly on the speech," Cotton said. "I was taking a nap and I missed it." He was, to be sure, about to retire from politics and had nothing to lose, but this may have been Cotton's greatest public service. He lighted a way that others, if they but will, can follow. NBC News correspondent Welles Hangen, missing since the fighting in Cambodia in 1970, had an unrivaled gift for the succinctness that is part of a civil tongue. Each year NBC correspondents tour the country in a group, appearing in public and answering questions from members of the audiences. In 1961, when India invaded what was then Portuguese Goa, Welles was NBC's correspondent in New Delhi. During that year's tour somebody sent up a one-word question: "Goa?" Welles gave a one-word answer: "Gone." At the Democratic convention in 1976, a reporter asked Amy Carter, eight-year-old daughter of Rosalynn and Jimmy, whether she had a message for the children of America. Said Amy: "No."

In the summer of 1960 I went to Sauk Center, Minnesota, for a television story about a festival honoring Sinclair Lewis, who was born there. One day a local resident said of a task that was facing us, "It's more than the horse can pull." We city boys thought that amusingly bucolic, but in seven words it's hard to say more. During an American Federation of Television and Radio Artists strike against NBC in April 1967, I was on the picket line, shortening my life inhaling the carbon monoxide fumes on Sixth Avenue,* when an NBC executive, a friend, walked by. "Bolshevik scum," he said cheerily. It made the day. In May 1960 the Big Four (Eisenhower, Khrushchev, de Gaulle, Macmillan) meeting in Paris broke up when Francis Gary Powers and his U-2 aircraft were shot down over the Soviet Union. I was NBC's Paris correspondent at the time, and when the conference ended I was among the reporters questioning Charles E. Bohlen, one of Eisenhower's chief advisers. A reporter asked Ambassador Bohlen whether the U-2 would be used again. Bohlen looked at him with mild impatience. "It is a blown instrument," he said. Five words. A complete answer.

---

* Officially it is the Avenue of the Americas, and there is an equestrian statue of Simón Bolívar at the northern end to prove it. Most New Yorkers say Sixth Avenue. It is hard to imagine anyone getting into a taxi and saying, "Fifty-second Street and the Avenue of the Americas, and hurry!"

I remember, decades ago, listening to Claude Pepper, then a senator from Florida, defending his vote on a civil rights issue that split him away from other Southern Democrats. Pepper has not been one of the most memorable of twentieth-century politicians, but he has always been an effective speaker. "I will not vote to stultify the Constitution of the United States," he said. Plainly phrased, but eloquent.

American English, drawing on so many regional differences, so many immigrant groups, and such a range of business, farming, industrial, athletic, and artistic experiences, can have an incomparable richness. Instead, high crimes and misdemeanors are visited upon it, and those who commit them do not understand that they are crimes against themselves. The language belongs to all of us. We have no more valuable possession.

Foreigners often have a peculiar talent for using English in an original way. After an earthquake in the North of Italy in the spring of 1976, a local resident described the scene. "Dogs were complaining," he said, "and animals were shouting." I am trying not to shout but I am complaining. Civilly. Most of the time.

# A One-Way Streetcar
# Named Detente

The rangy Texan had a sprawling ranch of his own, and his parents lived in a sprawling red brick building in a sprawling retirement community he often visited, so he felt not out of place on the sprawling game reserve where he had gone to pick off a trophy or two among the game animals with which he hoped to establish an adversary relationship. He wondered who his companions on the safari would be, and he had not long to wait. There was a hesitant, almost furtive knock at the door. Throwing it open, the Texan recognized a former Greek strongman.

"How are you, old buddy?" the Texan asked rangily.

"Not so well," the Greek replied.

"Anything specific? Any symptoms?"

"Well," the Greek said, "when I flex my muscles, nothing happens. They don't bulge."

Two military men followed in his wake. One was Admiral Isaac Kidd, known to the columnist Jack Anderson as the bluff head of Navy matériel; the other, Juan Velasco Alvarado, known to the *New York Times* as Peru's feisty army strongman. Kidd at once said something bluff about naval vessels. "When they break," he said, "I fix them." Velasco tried to say something feisty, but he was still bemused by his forcible retirement in August 1975. He looked about spiritedly, then fixed his eyes on the Greek and said, "I can lick any strongman in the house."

"You have the advantage of me, sir," the Greek replied. "I am a mere shadow of my former self. A few years ago it might have been different, before the foundations of my repressive regime tottered."

Velasco softened. "What happened?" he asked.

"The commonly accepted explanation," the Greek said, "is that I was chosen because my associates thought I would be a pliable figurehead. However, I turned into a firm, strong-willed ruler and sometimes lashed out at my cowed subordinates. The result was that after high-level discussion, far-reaching debate and last-ditch negotiations, followed by a spate of rumors, I was assailed as one who would turn the revolution to his own ends, arrested in a predawn raid, and toppled by my disgruntled fellow plotters."

"Was it a bloodless coup," Velasco asked, "or were lifeless bodies seen?"

The Greek hung his head. "Bloodless," he said.

"Mine was too," Velasco said consolingly. He changed the subject. "I also take on erstwhile boy wonders. Any of them here?"

"Cut it out, Velasco," Admiral Kidd said. "Any erstwhile boy wonders who would come here are aging prime ministers by now, or aged former prime ministers. You wouldn't go after them."

"I suppose you're right," Velasco said, "but I might make an exception for the Kremlin's aging leadership."

The Texan intervened. "The Kremlin's aging leadership is not coming," he said. "Its members were last seen in public reviewing the troops on the anniversary of the Bolshevik Revolution, standing on top of the refurbished Lenin Mausoleum wearing overcoats and heavy capes against a cold rain. The Chinese, who never spoke of the aging Kremlin leaders because of frail eighty-two-year-old Chairman Mao, described them as the Soviet revisionist leading clique, whose naked policy of colonial expansion was evidence of the new Tsars' feverish quest for world hegemony.* They also predicted that rightist deviationists would be smashed in their bourgeois headquarters by the torrent of the revolutionary mass movement.

"That shook the Kremlin's aging leaders," the Texan explained, "because they had themselves just finished administering a resolute rebuff to bourgeois falsifiers who seize upon any fabrication in their blind hatred for the future of all mankind. The aging leaders therefore went to the beautiful former imperial capital, Leningrad, where they could be protected by the vaunted power of the KGB."

"Is anybody ailing coming?" Velasco asked.

"Probably not," the Texan replied. "Reservations were made for an ailing chief of state and his aides, but they were canceled."†

---

* The Soviet and Chinese governments have a way of insulting each other that is peculiarly their own. You seek hegemony, the Chinese will tell the Russians. You seek hegemony, the Russians will tell the Chinese. In the 1950s some of us on the outside thought that the two governments might be seeking hegemony together, but their paths parted. Ever since, according to the Chinese, the Russians have been looking for hegemony high and low and in every nook and cranny, while according to the Russians the Chinese are obsessed with hegemony and think of nothing else except, in lighter moments, inciting a third world war. An unnamed Pakistani has told the *New York Times,* "The Indians have been bitten by the bug of wanting hegemony of the subcontinent." The *Times* found an Indian to deny it. The hegemoniacal debate goes on.

† Aides are used by aideworthy people not only for the obvious purpose—providing aid—but for the sake of journalists who find aides handy for hanging unattributable quotations on. *Time* magazine knows the location of more Washington aides than any other news organization and even used one to hang an unattributed murmur on: " 'That was really rough,' one of Ford's aides murmured."

When a politician acquires a number of aides, he has an entourage. Entourage members open doors, are brisk but friendly, and look as though they are standing by to be consulted on difficult questions. This

"Is there at least somebody coming from an ailing UN agency?"

"No."

"Why not?"

"Because the ailing agency is pulling in its belt and can't afford it."

"Explain something to me. I read in one of your papers about the ailing Daniel P. Moynihan. Is that a person or a position?"

"In a sense it is both, because although there is a Daniel P. Moynihan, it is also true that if there weren't he would have had to be invented."

"Is that because diplomacy is too serious a matter to be left to the diplomats?"

The Texan nodded.

"Moynihan has nonetheless left it to the diplomats."

The Texan nodded again. "An oversight," he said.

Here we leave the rangy Texan, the bluff head of Navy matériel, and the former Greek and Peruvian strongmen, though they will be back with further adventures at the end of this chapter. I want to pause here to consider how our ranches came to be sprawling and our language in politics and foreign affairs so burdened by clichés that thought about them is almost ruled out.*

---

is not so easy as it sounds, because if the entourage member ever seems to be at loose ends or superfluous, he runs the risk of appearing to be a hanger-on. The hanger-on's position is not official; he is not on the payroll, or even on a per diem; and his hold is precarious. One rarely hears the term hanger-on without mere before it. That implies contempt, and nobody turns up at somebody's campaign headquarters and says, "I'm applying for a job as hanger-on." However, for the hanger-on of accomplishment, there is always the possibility of promotion if an opening should turn up in the entourage.

* By the same process, the dust jacket of *Strictly Speaking* credited me with having anchored NBC's coverage of various events. "I missed your broadcasts and would be much obliged if you would send me a diagram showing how you anchored the coverage," wrote Jacob L. Fox of Chicago. "A weighty assignment, no doubt," wrote Conrad Teitell from his law office in New York. Very weighty.

In foreign affairs, for example, it has long been almost impossible to go beyond the question of whether, in its relations with the Soviet Union, the United States is on a one-way street or a two-way street, and whether it even knows the difference.

I used to think that glory awaited the politician who took the next logical step and said that détente must not be allowed to become a dead-end street, but President Ford may have put an end to that possibility. Soon after Ronald Reagan pronounced détente a one-way street—connecting the New Hampshire and Massachusetts primaries—Ford announced that détente was "only a word that was coined" and that he would not use it because it was no longer "applicable." Instead, Ford said, "I think what we ought to say is that the United States will meet with superpowers—the Soviet Union, China and others—and seek to relax tensions so that we can continue a policy of peace through strength."

Because in diplomacy détente means a relaxation of tensions, it appears that everybody was so busy looking for hidden significance in the President's remark that nobody thought of asking him who the other superpowers were. There were none. It is my guess that there was also no hidden significance. Ford was tired of hearing that he had been seen on a one-way street consorting with a foreign word of doubtful reputation. It is only a step from being seen on a one-way street in such company to being accused of détenting on the old camp ground, which would be sacrilege. However, nobody can say, "Seeking to relax tensions so as to continue a policy of peace through strength is a one-way street." Ford outwitted his rival.

Jimmy Carter, coming late to these matters, pronounced détente a two-way street but also asked that if we travel down the nuclear road we do so with our eyes wide open.* Open eyes are advisable on all thoroughfares, and Carter was not thought to have made an original contribution to arms control theory and practice.

---

\* Look down, look down, that nuclear road, before you travel on.

Leonid Brezhnev, although he was also taking part in détente, was not having the problems that Ford was. For one thing, the Soviet Ministry of One-Way Street Construction has been in existence for a long time and is the most experienced ministry of its kind in the world. There is no equivalent in the United States. We have not even had any proposals to divert money from the federal highway fund for the purpose, whereas the Russians divert money from one of their dearest projects, toiling masses transit. So in his keynote speech to the Congress of the Soviet Communist party in Moscow, Brezhnev was able to say, "We make no secret of the fact that we see détente as the way to create more favorable conditions for peaceful socialist and Communist construction." From Ford's point of view, Brezhnev might have done better to keep it a secret, since the President's critics insisted that all of that construction, the nature of which the wily Brezhnev did not specify, came down to laying out and paving you know what.

I must say that all this left me puzzled. If peace and security lie at both ends of a two-way street, as they must—after all, if both nations are going in the same direction on a two-way street, they might just as well be on a one-way street—why bother to leave your end for the other? Moreover, if eyeball-to-eyeball confrontations are to be avoided, the one-way street seems to be the place to avoid them. On a one-way street, all traffic moves in the same direction, and unless somebody is walking backward no one's eyeball can come flush against anyone else's. Simply stated, a one-way street is not what Henry Kissinger would call a context of confrontation, and that is the context eyeball-to-eyeball requires. The confrontation states of the Middle East, subsidized by their oil-rich neighbors, follow a confrontational strategy, and are the owners of some of the most bellicose eyeballs now on view. Yet they sedulously avoid one-way streets. So do the developing nations Kissinger himself has said constitute "a rigid, ideological, confrontationist coalition of their own." They know that it is on a two-way street that even an innocuous bilateral meeting may turn sinister—a turn to the left on a two-way street—when the eyeballs are barely in range. That is why they are often seen lounging on two-way street corners, looking for trouble. Multilateral eyeball-to-eyeball confrontations are, by definition, impossible.

I hope that this information will be reassuring to Senator Lowell Weicker of Connecticut. Weicker has been worried lest a mistaken policy on energy result in our being confronted with a confrontation. Not if you take the right road. It should also reassure our allies in Western Europe, who want arms standardized in the North Atlantic Treaty Organization and who, because they don't want to buy everything here while we buy nothing there, would like the transactions carried out on a two-way street. They should forget the streets. A broad avenue of cooperation is what they should have in mind.

Because of the preoccupation with streets, broad avenues of cooperation have not been much talked about of late, but they lead, all being well, to the broad sunlit uplands of peace and plenty to which, at the end of many of his speeches, Winston Churchill used to see humanity advancing. It always came as a shock to me when, sitting in the House of Commons press gallery in the 1950s, I would hear jeers going up from the Labour side as Churchill approached his peroration and took off. Some of this was simple partisanship: they were Labourites and Churchill was the leader of the Conservatives. But it was also caused by their knowing what was coming—oratorical flourishes, an inspirational ending, an attempt to equal some of the great phrases spoken ten and fifteen years before. Churchill was more effective away from the sunlit uplands and when he was at his most concrete. "Jaw, jaw," he once said about talking to the Russians, "is better than war, war." An argument cannot be put better than that.

A few years later one of Churchill's successors as prime minister, Harold Macmillan, tried a variation on it. "There ain't," he said, "gonna be no war." Coming from a man of his fusty appearance, it was brilliantly effective in turning debate on foreign affairs into the channel where Macmillan wanted it. Language is a marvelous servant for those who know how to use it. In 1958 a revolt in Algeria by French colonists and military men who wanted Algeria to remain French restored Charles de Gaulle to power in Paris. De Gaulle went to Algiers and, from the balcony overlooking the Place du Gouvernement-Général, where all the huge rallies had taken place, spoke to those who had brought about his return. *"Je vous ai compris,"* he told them. "I have understood you." Applause, cheers, exultation. The phrase could not have been more carefully chosen. The unspoken part of it was, "Yes, and you're not going to get what you want." What de Gaulle did say quieted the storm. A few years later, Algeria was independent. Was it fair? Perhaps not. But as an effective use of language, it has rarely been equaled.*

I remember some effective language being used on me at that time. During the uprising I went to Radio Algiers to broadcast to the United States. American policy was not popular with those in revolt. A soldier with a rifle blocked my way. *"Vous êtes Americain?"* he asked. I said I was. *"Prenez la porte,"* he said, literally "Take the door" and unmistakably "Get out."

Four years later I was in Vietnam talking to a South Vietnamese colonel about the strategic villages and hamlets plan. This involved placing the peasants in fortified areas from which they would go forth to the fields in the morning and to which they would return to be sealed off from the Communists at night. The colonel, later killed in mysterious circumstances while trying to seize power, said, "They're not locking the Communists out. They're locking the Communists in." It was a precise measure of what was happening, and a precise explanation of why the plan failed.

Talk about contexts of confrontation and two-way streets,

---

* De Gaulle, by the way, could speak English. When he visited the United States at the end of 1959, I went along, as NBC's Paris correspondent, to help in the coverage. There was a reception at the French Embassy, and as I approached de Gaulle I saw one of his associates nudge him and tell him I was there. He looked down at me and said, "I am very happy to see you here." Whether he spoke in English because he was in Washington and thought it fitting or did not want to provoke me into speaking French, I never knew.

its banality apart, makes discussion of foreign affairs and politics empty. It substitutes stereotypes for thought. It reduces discussion to an exchange of catch phrases. We are caught between one-way street slogans on one side and communiqué language on the other.

In November of 1974, President Ford went to Japan, a visit that, whatever else it may have achieved, produced a compendium of communiqué language not surpassed before or since. The communiqué contained—here you proceed at your own risk and probably would be well advised to have a companion—friendly and cooperative relations, harmonious relations, constructive relations, cooperative relations, the totality of varied relationships, a close and mutually beneficial relationship based on the principle of equality (it's only the beginning, folks, only the beginning), a common determination, an enhanced scope for creativity, the maintenance of peace and the evolution of a stable international order, peaceful settlement of outstanding issues, sustained and orderly growth, contributions made in the light of responsibilities and capabilities, an effective and meaningful role, dedicated efforts, coordinated responses, intensified efforts, close cooperation, growing interdependence, global economic difficulties (about halfway there now), the constructive use of human and material resources, an open and harmonious world economic system, constructive participation, a stable and balanced international monetary order, more efficient and rational utilization and distribution of world resources, enhanced cooperation, further international cooperative efforts, a new era of creativity and common progress, constructive participation in multilateral efforts, the well-being of the peoples of the world (hang on), a steady improvement in technological and economic capabilities, a common concern, sound and orderly growth, new challenges common to mankind, broad cooperation, mutual understanding and enhanced communication, the expansion of cultural and educational interchange, the spirit of mutual friendship and trust, frank and timely consultations, potential bilateral issues, pressing global problems of common concern (nearly home), many diverse fields of human endeavor, major foundation stones, an indispensable element, a new page in the history of amity, and a promise to go on striving steadily to encourage a further relaxation of tensions in the world through dialogue and exchanges with countries of different social systems. (Author! Author!)

The Tokyo communiqué somehow left out resolute action, which governments often promise to take at the end of meaningless meetings. Otherwise it is the Sistine Chapel of communiqués. It said what was to be said on the subject forever, and no more communiqués need be issued. Instead, the most-favored-nation technique used in trade could be applied. We would offer any friendly country the same terms that were given to Japan— harmonious, constructive, stable, rational, enhanced, steady, broad, frank, timely, mutual, and the rest. New pages in the history of amity could be turned over at will.

It will be recalled that we left diplomacy in the streets and our minds in the gutter. Let us say that an eyeball-to-eyeball confrontation has taken place, possibly on a street temporarily closed for repairs. In the classic case, it will turn into a head-to-head summit, though this requires some contortion and agility on both sides and, when aging leaders are involved, as they often are, cannot always be arranged.

The *New York Times* columnist William Safire spotted one head-to-head summit at which four eyes were looking at each other but only two eyes met. This may happen with experienced politicians, who appear to be considering the immediate situation but actually have already sized it up and have one eye on the future. It may also be caused by that scourge of American life, irregularity, which leads the mind to wander. The irregular one may be looking at you and apparently concentrating on what you are saying, but his mind is on something else.

Sometimes there is an intermediate step between confrontation and summit, between eyeball-to-eyeball and head-to-head. This is taken when one of the parties to the confrontation says challengingly and perhaps with a slight sneer, "How about a little poker? Diplomatic poker, I mean." The other is nothing loath (sometimes, indeed, he is ailing Prime Minister Nothing Loath) and the game is on. The principal problem in arranging a diplomatic poker game used to be finding a suitable location, since the participants may bring along as bargaining chips intercontinental ballistic missiles, advanced industrial bases, and burgeoning farm production, and much space is needed to stack them. This is no longer a problem, since it is widely understood that the game will take place either in "the gray area between foreign policy and overt commitment" that Henry Kissinger spoke of in a speech at the University of Wyoming at Laramie, or the "twilight area between tranquility and open confrontation" that he identified in a speech to the Institute of Strategic Studies in London.* Almost everybody knows where to find the gray area. It is out-of-doors, under a heavy cloud cover, and on an intersection between a one-way street and a two-way street. The twilight area is the next area over. Sometimes disputes arise over which is to be used, but the twilight area is open for only a couple of hours a day and has to be booked in advance, so the gray area gets most of the games. Visibility is not good in either.

In spite of its menacing ring, eyeballing is not always hostile. In December 1974 the Democrats held a midterm convention in Kansas City. Members of Senator Henry Jackson's staff chose groups of ten to fifteen delegates and led them off the floor for what one of Jackson's assistants called "an eyeball-to-eyeball"

---

* As Kissinger's reputation declined, so did his language. It became harder for him to convince Congress and the people that his policies were correct and that he was still a miracle man as advertised, and he began to use the language he heard around him. Discussing his warning to Cuba against further military activities in Africa after the intervention in Angola, Kissinger told the Senate Foreign Relations Committee: "We should not look at the immediate situation in terms of planning a new move in any time frame that is now immediately foreseeable." In the speech at Laramie, however, he foresaw a time frame in which the United States might "become an isolated fortress island in a hostile and turbulent global sea." An isolated island, as noted elsewhere, is a peculiarly lonely place to be, but for the United States to become one would require more cooperation than Mexico and Canada are likely to offer. The global sea, a perfectly round body of water, has so far been produced only under laboratory conditions.

with the Senator. That meant that the delegates were allowed to be close to Jackson and to converse with him without an intermediary and to judge the stuff of which he was then made.

This kind of eyeball-to-eyeballing, though often amiable, should not be confused with eyeballing, eyeball analysis, or eye contact. The baritone Sherrill Milnes has told an interviewer that he is able to sing a score after eyeballing it. The action here is unilateral. The score does not eyeball back. Eyeball analysis takes place when archeologists dig up artifacts and look at them with the naked eye. However, most archeologists consider it infra dig and prefer to use instruments, even though it was *on* an infra dig that one of the most important infrastructures of an ancient civilization was found.

Eye contact comes from television, and it occurs when a broadcaster is courageous enough to look up from the script and into the camera lens. This requires that the broadcaster have confidence that when he looks down again he will be able to find his place in the script or, lacking such confidence, be willing to risk it. You will hear it said of someone particularly adept at this, "Boy, has he got eye contact!" In the elections of November 1974, Governor Francis Sargent of Massachusetts, though he lost to Michael Dukakis, exhibited, according to the *New York Times,* "a folksy, grinning, hand-shaking, hugging style that won him the admiration of professional politicians, who said that he could lead a parade and make 'eye contact' with everyone in the crowd." Sargent, of course, with no script to follow, could concentrate on eye contact alone, and it must have helped, since late in the campaign he came from a long way back and almost won. This may start a new form of competition for votes among politicians, in which they no longer make promises or issue position papers or even make speeches, but simply go out and look citizens squarely in the eye. "Come to the speakin'," Lyndon Johnson used to tell voters when he campaigned. "Come to the eyeballin'," he would be saying now.

In television, a broadcaster need never look down at his script at all if a Teleprompter with a script on it is placed in front of the lens. However, one not skilled in its use may appear to be peering, mesmerized, into space. This does not count as eye contact. Sometimes the Teleprompter is placed above the lens, which calls for still more skill in looking up while not appearing to look up. A viewer sent me a drawing showing my eyes virtually all whites and pupils disappearing northward. This also would not count as eye contact.

It does not count as dialogue, either, that being what a politician who cannot think of anything else to issue clarion calls for issues clarion calls for. "We need," he says, "a dialogue."* This means that he is being constructive. Rhetoric is used when a politician wants to dismiss some argument or proposal as not constructive, and to convey a tone of tolerant contempt. "This," he says, "is rhetoric." Calls for dialogue are not dismissed as rhetoric. If they were, political life in the United States would come to an end. Dialogues recently recommended to us would have engaged developed and developing nations, producing and consuming nations, labor and management, President and Congress, East and West, North and South, and would have been meaningful, true, patient, honest, responsible, and conducted in a conducive atmosphere. There would also have been a natural gas dialogue at the request of the Pennsylvania Chamber of Commerce.

The *New York Times* asked for a dialogue on oil in an editorial in which it had the oil-consuming nations biting the bullet of pride and moving toward a common energy policy, while the oil-producing nations bit the apple of wisdom and planned to meet at the summit. Biting an apple smacks less of hysteria than biting a bullet, and this, as well as their possession of oil, explains why the OPEC countries have lately been so successful. In February 1975, twelve Senators and seventy Representatives asked President Ford for a serious, unemotional dialogue on getting the United States out of Indochina. They should have asked for eighty-two dialogues.

---

* This information has only recently been declassified: A dialogue consists of meaningful initiatives followed by a constructive response.

It is curious, this devotion to dialogue. An Army officer involved in the clemency program, Major General Eugene Forrester, told *People* magazine that he and his nineteen-year-old son had had "extremely volatile dialogue over Vietnam." He apparently meant that they had shouted at each other. A television executive made a speech in which he urged upon his listeners the virtues of a mutual dialogue together. The dialogue umbrella is broad. An interior decorating company in Lawrence, New York, is called Dialogue International Limited. An associate director of the Jewish Defense League, Dov Fisch, announced that the League would be sending some of its members "to engage in dialogues with Soviet diplomats as they emerge from the mission. We used to call it harassing," Fisch explained, "but harassing is illegal." Would that dialogue were.

Since editorials are unsigned, I do not know who composed the *Times*'s call for a dialogue on oil. It may have been Leonard Silk, a member of the paper's editorial board, who asked about a meeting between rich and poor nations in Paris, "Will Paris Talks Produce Dialogue?" How could they not? Or it may have been correspondent Charles Mohr, who in an article from Johannesburg reported that Prime Minister John Vorster of South Africa had "conducted a growing dialogue with some domestic black leaders." Mohr added that Vorster did this even though "Superimposed on the entire situation is the dead weight of an ideology of racial separation that has handcuffed many politicians and convinced many South Africans that there is no need to disengage from what one concerned Afrikaner had called 'an insufferable status quo.' " No one can disengage from a status quo when he is handcuffed by an ideology's dead weight, unless he gets help. This is exactly what a growing dialogue is intended to provide.

Other evidence suggests that the *Times*'s editorial on oil was written by a reporter named Steven R. Weisman, who in a review of a book called *The Real America* wrote that "it merits full recognition as a major contribution to the nation's political dialogue," one reason it merited that recognition being the fact that its author, Ben Wattenberg, had "limned a remarkable portrait of the American people." I did not know that anyone any longer limned, even columnists, and even while making a major contribution to the nation's political dialogue, which needs all the major contributions it can get. Limned?* I thought it had gone the way of lambent and plangent.

In February 1975 *Time* magazine had this to say about disagreements in Washington over energy and the economy: "For all the rhetorical smoke, the President and the Democrats are not that far apart on many other aspects of the program." Rhetorical smoke was used by American Indians when sending up signals that needed no answer, i.e., required no dialogue. *Time* may, however, have had a different source of the phrase in mind, the well-known saying, Where there is smoke, people are far apart.

King Hussein of Jordan said in April 1976 that any political changes in Lebanon should come about not through violence but through dialogue. Hussein was in Washington at the time as the guest of President Ford, which was appropriate because Ford is unusually fond of dialogue. Soon after taking office he called for a new dialogue with the nations of Latin America, though most of those nations were not aware that the old dialogue had ended, or even begun. Later, Ford called for a deepening dialogue with the nations of Latin América. Until then I had thought that a deepening dialogue took place between two men who talked to each other while digging a hole.

When Ford was involved in two shooting incidents late in 1975, he said that he did not want to cut down on his public appearances because he wanted to continue his "dialogue with the American people." Plunging into a crowd to shake hands is not a dialogue. Nor is making a speech. There has to be someone talking back. The twelfth annual America-Israel Dialogue was held in Jerusalem in June 1976. The former Israeli foreign min-

---

* In the course of his limning, Wattenberg, relying heavily on attitudinal surveys, found that "The dominant rhetoric of our time is a rhetoric of failure, guilt and crisis." Attitudinal surveys often lead to platitudinal conclusions.

ister, Abba Eban, said, "We must talk in full mutuality." That's a dialogue. Dialogue offers an excellent example of what is happening to the language. It is a word with a specific meaning in books, plays, moving pictures. That meaning is being lost, as governments embark on a policy of dialogue and the editorial writers follow along, urging a policy of dialogue on those governments that unaccountably don't already have one.

The State Department, announcing the appointment of an official to represent consumer rights and interests within the Department, promised "to take those steps necessary and feasible to promote and channel these rights and interests with respect to the maintenance and expansion of an international dialogue and awareness." Somebody was paid to write that. Before Morocco took over the Spanish Sahara, the Moroccan foreign minister went to Madrid to discuss the issue in, as he put it, "a spirit of dialogue." That is better than going in a spirit of monologue, but we are seeing dialogue taking on a mystical, magical quality, as though it meant more than a couple of people talking to each other, and as though a dialogue in itself were a solution.

Dialogue has become so ubiquitous that when, in October 1974, the Guards units in Whitehall in London returned to the saddle after three weeks on foot because their horses had had sore throats, it occurred to me that the sore throats had been caused by too much neigh-saying in the equine dialogue.

The deepening dialogue with the nations of Latin America that President Ford hankered after should be distinguished from the discussion in depth. The deepening dialogue is conducted on land, the in-depth discussion in water. On December 31, 1975, the White House announced that Prime Minister Yitzhak Rabin of Israel would visit Washington on January 27 so that he and President Ford could "discuss in depth the situation in the Middle East." The White House deputy press secretary, John Carlson, did not say what the depth would be, and speculation was, as it so often is, rife. Would Ford and Rabin duck their heads beneath the surface of the White House pool and exchange signals? Snorkel?

Don divers' gear* and go full fathom five into the Potomac? Would each board a submarine, have the skipper pass the order, "Take her down," and communicate by radio? Would they, mocking the dismay of the security men responsible for their safety, descend to a level that, so far as was known, had been reached only once before? (This was when federal officials carried out what one of them—he did not permit mention of his name—called "a very, very in-depth study" of the condition of New York City banks at the time the city was threatening to default on its debts. The officials were brought back by easy stages to avoid the bends.)

In the event, Rabin and Ford did none of these things— perhaps Carlson was misinformed—and I concluded that they had at most a shallow discussion. It was hardly worth Rabin's while coming over.

What has happened to some of our other old favorites since last we met—major, constituency, controversial, parameter, hopefully, and the rest? All have extended their reach. Thus, controversial. *Time* reported that "the delegates to an unusual General Congregation that is charting the controversial future course of the Jesuits voted to change policy on the papal vow." Evidently the Jesuits decided earlier that their future course would be controversial and the delegates were arranging it.

When President Ford went to Japan in 1974, his trousers aroused some unfavorable comment. Mrs. Ford, who did the President's packing, said that she had followed instructions in "a booklet on clothes and accessories" put out by Brooks Brothers. Brooks Brothers' manager in Washington, Robert Mallon, denied this. "We supplied the coat only—the coat only—plus the ascot and shoes," he said. "The controversial trousers belong to the President." The White House later explained that the controversial trousers had been left over from "an inauguration." Ford undoubtedly hoped that he would hear no more about them, and wore nonpartisan trousers from then on.

Nonetheless, there are politicians who might have envied

---

* Gear is always donned. It is never put on.

Ford the trousers and their grip on public attention. The mayor of Utica, New York, Ed Hanna, employs a public relations firm to advise the press that he is "available for interviews upon request," that he and "his frenetic populist regime have been flailing at tradition," that the heart of his plans for Utica is "the La Promenade re-development project," which would have an art center, antique shops, a crafts unit, apartments, and unusual boutique stores, and that in Mayor Hanna's view, "The phonies and the bluebloods and the politicians, who gave this city the name 'Sin City,' have been draining this lousy town too long." A press release describes Hanna as "New York State's Most Controvertial Mayor." This is not quite right. He is not the most controvertial mayor. He is the only one. For Mayor Hanna, man of the La Promenade project, controvertial is the le mot juste.

As controversial has extended its reach, so has alleged. When a House committee decided to publish a report on United States intelligence activities, White House press secretary Ron Nessen said, "Under the agreement, the President should have had a chance to review the classified material in the report before it was leaked to the public. The President views with the most serious concern the leak of the alleged contents of the report." A leak of alleged contents is itself only an alleged leak until it is determined that the contents are the genuine contents. As alleged. The New Haven, Connecticut, *Register* began a story from Hamden, Connecticut: "It doesn't pay to allegedly attempt to remove auto parts from Chet's Auto Parts, Inc., 87 Welton St. Two young men found that out this week." Crime doesn't allegedly pay.

Convince to, as in *New York* magazine's "Phyllis convinced Ford to join her on an expedition to a ski resort" and United Press International's "Five bandits convinced a Brink's armored car driver to open his truck door by pointing a 50MM anti-aircraft gun at him,"* has expanded in three ways. First, people may now be convinced not to.

---

* A .38-caliber revolver was known as a convincer in the gangster talk of the thirties. Imagine how convincing an antiaircraft gun must be.

"Kansas City, Mo. (UPI)—Democratic National Chairman Robert Strauss said he doubted if reform delegates could have been convinced not to walk out of a weekend meeting to plan the party's December miniconvention."

People may now also be convinced into.

From an article in the *New York Times* travel section by a senior editor of a large New York publishing house:

"Here is where we will make love," Antonio said. "Now you will take off your suit."

"Listen, Antonio, I told you no," I insisted. "Do you really think I'm saying it just so I can let you convince me into saying yes? I'm not like that. I say what I mean and I mean no."

He shrugged his shoulders. "It is time to eat now. Give me the plastic bag."

From the resignation expressed by Antonio, driven though he was to eating a plastic bag in frustration, we may conclude that people may not only be convinced into doing something, they may also be convinced out of it.

Lengthy brief, as in "The defense attorney submitted a lengthy brief in support of his motion," has not done well. The prosecuting attorney of Allen County, Ohio, Lawrence S. Huffman, closed a moving picture theater in Lima, Ohio, as a public nuisance on the ground that it showed obscene films. The order was overturned in court, and Huffman asked the United States Supreme Court to reverse that. He submitted a lengthy brief in which the statement of facts covered nineteen pages and the legal arguments eighty-three more. The Supreme Court told him to make his lengthy brief less lengthy and more brief or it would not listen to his argument.

Constituency, as in "He is building a constituency among the poor and disadvantaged," has lost standing also. It now takes supportive before it, or broad-based. Broad-based constituencies are extremely difficult to build because they are made up of people who are continually on the move, usually in wide-bodied comfort on American Airlines or on TWA's widebody 1011 service between New York and Los Angeles.

Confrontation, referred to earlier, appears to be strong, but the expert eye can detect a slight crack, a fraying. This appeared with the first mention of direct confrontations, which implied that there could be confrontations of secondary and tertiary kinds. C. L. Sulzberger has written in the *New York Times* about a friendly confrontation between the Swedish and Yugoslav versions of socialism. All this threatens so to cheapen confrontations that no self-respecting government will want to have one.

Somewhat the same thing is happening to parameter. Although at times the entire nation appears to be running in a hundred-parameter dash, parameter is shrinking or narrowing and may eventually disappear. Jules Power, executive producer of ABC's "AM America," wrote that "There are fairly narrow parameters as to what one can and cannot do" in the Soviet Union. The journalism review *More* sighted narrow parameters in this country, these being the parameters of debate over energy policy in the United States. The Institute for American Strategy accused CBS News of reporting in a partial and slanted way and so of "narrowing the parameters of public debate" on national defense. That is impossible, but CBS denied it anyway.

David Halberstam, writing in the *Atlantic,* recalled Edward R. Murrow's becoming a tough-minded correspondent on the domestic scene after the Second World War and creating tension that "quickly marked the parameters of freedom within broadcasting in the 1950's." By 1960, according to Halberstam, Murrow saw broadcasting becoming "more and more a vehicle for manipulation rather than a vehicle for broadening the parameters of vision." Murrow opened the door of the vehicle and got out, and the flags flying at the parameter line were taken down.

Parameter was not around in Murrow's time. He would not have used it if it had been. It is true, of course, that in those days the parametric pressure was not so strong as it is now. Now the State Department, according to its public announcements, thinks nothing of looking within itself for action parameters and finding them along with improved linkages and a broad spectrum, which make up an impressive bonus.

The *New York Times* reported that labor and management were working out the economic parameters of a settlement. Later, President Ford welcomed those parameters as falling "within the parameters of what we would call a defendable agreement." (The Council of Economic Advisers mans the parapets.) The *Times*'s business page one day set out the parameters for the new magazine *People*—among them that it have single-copy sales only, reach a high female audience with reasonably high demographs, and have a good pass-along audience. Reasonably high demographs means that the magazine's readers fall within an age group, usually the early twenties to the mid-forties, that does a good deal of buying. It will be recognized at once as a parameter. (Demographic increments, which sound somewhat the same, are not parameters. Demographic increment is a social science term for an addition to a population. Demographs within demographic increments would vary.) In a good pass-along audience, those who have read the magazine pass it along a straight and narrow path to people who have not. It is the domino theory of circulation.

Hopefully—as in "Hopefully, this afternoon the fog will lift and we can get out there with a helicopter" (from the United States Coast Guard in New Orleans); "Hopefully it is a shorter-range evil" (President Ford); "I am happily and hopefully going to shut off their federal funds" (Madalyn Murray O'Hair, opponent of prayer in the schools); and "Hopefully the dead man will float to the surface* after about ten days" (author unknown)—has hopelessly infected other words heretofore immune. I have, for example, seen an advertisement for a California Riesling that was "regretfully available only in very limited quantities." That is the hopefully disease spreading, but no variation is likely to approach the majesty of the announcement by the president of the Green Bay Packers, Dominic Olejniczak, when discussing the hiring of a new coach. "We hope," he said, "to have an announcement before the end of the week, hopefully before that."

This has been rivaled in my experience only by an application

---

* With the body badly decapitated.

of the foundation stone of American English, "Y'know." A friend in Detroit told me he had heard a colleague say, "Y'know, you never know."*

Inoperative, as in Ron Ziegler's announcement in April 1973 that his earlier statements on the Watergate affair were inoperative, has reached the construction industry. I live in midtown New York, near a site where a big new building recently went up. Projects of that size have public address systems for transmitting instructions, and one day I heard this: "Please use the inside elevators for going up in the building. The outside elevator is inoperative."

Unfortunately, I was not there when the announcement was made that the elevator was, in the Washington style, once again operational, which is Washington's way of saying that something is ready. Operational is just beginning to wrinkle from exposure to the elements. Its future is certain. It will be a cliché.

So will presence be a cliché. Presences are usually military. The United States had one in Thailand for twenty-six years, until in 1976 the presence became a thing of the past. Presence is a Washington word, so the British have picked it up. Said Lieutenant Colonel Robert Ward, commander of the First Regiment of the Queen's Dragoon Guards, stationed in Northern Ireland: "The first aim is to reassure the local populace of a maximum presence here."

We came, we saw, we established a maximum presence. The leaders of the victorious faction in the Angolan civil war told an assistant to Senator John Tunney of California, "We have no desire for a permanent Soviet or Cuban presence." They probably would have preferred to say that they did not want the Cubans and

---

* Hopefully has its academic supporters, who say that it is the equivalent of the German *hoffentlich*. However, Nicholas Christy, a professor of medicine at the College of Physicians and Surgeons of Columbia University, wrote to me that *hoffentlich* means it is to be hoped. The German for hopefully, he wrote, is *hoffnungsvoll*. Which leads me to say *hoffnungsvoll* that Americans, *hoffentlich*, will stop misusing hopefully.

Russians to stay but wanted to assure Washington on this point, since Washington obstinately believes that presence makes the heart grow fonder. They therefore put it into language the United States Government would understand.

As new clichés make their way in, often used incorrectly, serviceable old words make their way out. Ambivalent, which means having conflicting feelings—feelings, for example, of love and hate—is shoving ambiguous, which means uncertain or doubtful. Ambiguous should shove back. Consensus is coming in, and majority and agreement are going out. We are being told about a fair consensus, a strong consensus, a growing consensus, a solid consensus, a general consensus, a broad consensus. Jimmy Carter said about certain campaign issues, "You'll never get anybody to agree on them. You won't even get a consensus on them." A consensus is an opinion collectively held, and it either exists or it doesn't. It cannot be fair, meaning partial, and it must be general or it wouldn't be a consensus.

Consensus has obvious appeal. It is new and pompous, its meaning is not well understood, and its use makes public discussion less specific. It was bound to flourish. Consensus is not quite the biggest of the new clichés, however. Global is, and as it comes in, world and worldwide go out. Henry Kissinger speaks of maintaining a balance of global stability (balances of instability are notoriously hard to maintain) and of global peace. Kissinger also points out that "In the global dialogue among the industrial and developing worlds, the communist nations are conspicuous by their absence." Since the communist nations take up a large part of the globe, if they are absent the dialogue isn't global.

The commander of NATO forces in Europe, General Alexander Haig, sees the West confronted by a global Soviet military capability and wants the western nations to develop the ability (not capability?) to manage global Soviet power in a global sense. James Schlesinger, when he was Secretary of Defense, put it more succinctly. He worried about the global military equilibrium with the Soviet Union. (If you don't have it, there goes the globallgame.)

The United Nations General Assembly convokes a global conference on the consequences of the misuse of land. The consequences of that misuse, I am sorry to say, go under the name of desertification. A new book about multinational corporations is called *Global Reach*. A *Publishers Weekly* reviewer says that the heads of these corporations are global oligopolists and have global vision. Very broad parameters. In the press, the migration of wealth from one part of the world to another—after oil prices were raised, for example—is described as a global challenge, and there is much concern about global fallout, though how anything can fall out of the globe I do not see. Ronald Reagan accuses the Ford Administration of lacking a coherent global view, and Governor Edmund Brown, Jr., of California, known for a certain shyness, deprecatingly describes something he has said about the limits of natural resources as "a bit global." Later, Brown's organizers in the Oregon primary hold a strategy meeting in Portland in the Global Delicatessen, which, I take it, sells the world's wurst.

The Canadians, ever on the alert, ask: Can one of Canada's most successful international companies get global recognition with a name change? Their answer is yes, by changing its name from Northern Electric to Northern Telecom. An easier way would have been to broadcast on Canada's Global Television Network. As the old saying goes, it's a small globe.

Global was a cliché once before. During the Second World War, Franklin Roosevelt talked a great deal about global interests, global considerations, and global repercussions. The playwright Clare Boothe Luce, then a member of the House of Representatives, disagreed with much of what Roosevelt was saying. It was, she said, globaloney. It took global thirty years to recover.

The Canadians may find the corporate name change from Northern Electric to Northern Telecom counterproductive. That is another new cliché, used in place of self-defeating, unwise, misjudged, and foolish. Counterproductive is altogether larger than any of these, and more nearly official. In the medical world it has already spawned countertherapeutic. It sounds major.

Major itself is colossal. I have already mentioned major contributions to the nation's political dialogue. These might be encouraged by being made tax deductible. "Did you make any major contributions to the nation's political dialogue last year?" the question on the income tax form would say. "If so, write brief summaries of them in the space provided and attach receipts showing to whom they were made and your estimate of their value. When possible, estimates should be accompanied by documents, receipts, etc."*

The *New York Times* continues to be the great, or major, discoverer of the quality of majorness almost everywhere it looks, wholesale. Picking my way through the *Times*'s major jungle of major news stories of the day, past major tests, major enemy categories, major groups of prisoners, major western embassies, major roles, a major witness, a major theme, major social issues, major highway construction, a major setback, a major argument, major gains, a major realignment, major social and psychological implications, major rail lines, major fields, major bills, major elements, major progress, major states, a major war, major nationalist groups, major help, a major producer, a major case, major differences, major industrial powers, a major operation, major disasters, major banks, a once-major voice, a major spring season, and a major incident that might spark potentially explosive material, I came to two stories in which the *Times* surpassed itself. One came from Watergate days and contained a major task, a major event, major trials, major players, and major solid cases to be made against major figures. In the other story the *Times* showed what it could do with limited space in a front-page précis: "The first major revision of the city's new fire code for high-rise

---

* The Internal Revenue Service would have in mind here evidence that a contribution has been noticed and discussed and so deserves to be deemed major. Mention in a column by David Broder or Joseph Kraft or Evans and Novak would be considered conclusive proof. So would serving as the basis for a question on "Meet the Press" or the "Today" show. Being discussed by an aide to a candidate, and without attribution, would not by itself be enough.

office buildings, designed to remove a major cause of fire deaths, went into effect yesterday with the vast majority of buildings in noncompliance." The detailed story ran on a non-outside page, and in it the major revision and vast majority of buildings were joined by a major violator and a major factor. The *Times* is a major violator. I often wish it weren't. If a major boycott were imposed by the *Times* copy desk for one day's editions, the news would be fit to print, but couldn't be.

President Ford sent a message to Congress on energy in which he said,

"I have a very deep belief in America's capabilities. Within the next 10 years, my program envisions:

"200 major nuclear power plants.

"250 major new coal mines.

"150 major coal-fired power plants.

"30 major new refineries.

"20 major new synthetic fuel plants."

That was 650 majors. In major competition, that is known as throwing down the gauntlet, or as the galloping major.

Presidents have obvious advantages in these matters, but what counts is playing the game. The *Book-of-the-Month Club News* has described the publication of a book as "a major event," even without the assurance that the book would become a major motion picture. There is a Conference of Presidents of Major American Jewish Organizations. In November 1974 a Major Interdisciplinary Symposium on the Human Condition was held in Palm Coast, Florida. In February 1975 the San Francisco Board of Education voted to end public school sports as an economy measure, and Erv Delman, president of the San Francisco Coaches' Association, said, "This is catastrophic and major."

On December 10, 1974, the twenty-fifth anniversary of Chiang Kai-shek's arrival on Taiwan, the *New York Times* reported that "Few noticed and those who did averted their eyes as a major milestone in the history of this embattled island passed by today without commemorative speeches, editorials or public recognition of any kind." It is easy to see why the *Times* considered this news. A minor milestone might be expected to escape public attention, and the most it can hope for in the end probably is to be installed along the road to recovery in a once thriving hub of commerce, but a major milestone trudging by cries out not for averted eyes but for recognition.

"Who is that shrieking out there, Sergeant?"

"I believe it's Major Milestone, sir."

"Very well, Sergeant. Let him in."

"Yes, sir." (Salutes smartly and turns.) "Advance, Major Milestone, and be recognized."

The British, possibly because they want to go on being considered a major power, are making major their own. In early 1976, Iran had a budget deficit and began delaying payment for goods bought overseas. A British government official, asked about this, said that Iran had not done anything as serious as canceling a contract. "What we're looking for," he said, "is a major 'no' on a project that would point to a central government direction not to spend any more money." In a world in which people avert their eyes as major milestones pass by, a major no that points should not be impossible to find. It may well be found watching the march past of the major milestones and warning them away from paths down which they should not go.

Major milestones usually forage off the country, and they sometimes set up more or less permanent camp in the hope of becoming turning points. When they do, they may run into competition, especially in Washington, where most of the country's turning point production is concentrated. When President Ford signed his proposed budget for fiscal 1977 he said that he hoped it would be a turning point for the American people. More precisely, that is what he *would* have said a few years ago. However, the President knew that an unadorned turning point is ignored in Washington.* He therefore placed a major before it. Even then, Ford felt his phrase inadequate, since major turning points are claimed by people who are not even in the govern-

---

* "Why, it's just a little old turning point, son. We get 'em here all the time."

ment. When the Kentucky legislature defeated an attempt to rescind ratification of the Equal Rights Amendment, Liz Carpenter of ERAmerica, an organization in favor of ratification, said, "This represents a major turning point across the country for the equal rights. amendment." Ford therefore made his a very major turning point.

Nelson Rockefeller has helped to bring about the state of affairs in which major is routine and a turning point insignificant. In June 1975 a commission headed by Rockefeller and charged with investigating the CIA handed its report to President Ford. Rockefeller told reporters that the report would show that "There are things that have been done in contradiction to the statutes, but in comparison to the total effort, they are not major."

Senator Church of Idaho, chairman of a Senate committee investigating the CIA, objected that he had "hard evidence" that the CIA had been involved in murder plots, and said, "I do not regard murder plots as a minor matter."

Rockefeller replied that when he used the words "not major," he meant only the number of times the CIA broke the law,* not the seriousness of what it did. "I made no comment on seriousness," said Rockefeller. "I talked about magnitude." Magnitude means great size or extent, great importance or significance. Something of magnitude might once—come to a turning point, O Time, in thy flight—have been called major.

In the creation of old favorites, which is done by aging them prematurely, *Time* magazine has unrivaled resources. The tone is set at the top, as may be seen in the "Letter from the Publisher" in the issue of February 10, 1975, when the publisher, Ralph P. Davidson, wrote about a Middle East news tour by fifty-three United States businessmen, journalists, *Time* editors, and others.

After blinking at the distinction drawn between *Time* editors and journalists, I noted that the fifty-three tourists were citizens traveling at their own expense through an arena of world events. What kind of citizens? A practiced *Time* reader would know at once: Influential and concerned. What kind of arena? Crucial.

---

* A free translation by me of "done in contradiction to the statutes."

The "letter" contained no surprises. The tourists were given an opportunity (unique) to learn (firsthand) about a region (vital) by posing questions (hard) to Middle East kings, emirs, prime ministers, and presidents, to whom, during a round of interviews, dinners and seminars (busy), they were given access (well merited).

Were the tourists impressed? Deeply.

On the war-ravaged Golan Heights, how did the possibility of renewed fighting seem to them? Ominous.

And the current peace? Fragile.

The coffee in Saudi Arabia? Bitter.

The nations of the Persian Gulf? Rich.

No more?

Croesus-rich.

Another letter from the publisher described the cover story on the entertainer Cher by a contributor (prolific) who explored Hollywood's star syndrome (glittery), then drew on his experience (wide) for a story about the singer (slinky), who was interviewed on a day off (rare), while others made comments (candid).

A *Time* quiz:

In J. Edgar Hoover's last years as head of the FBI, what kind of head was he? Aging.

Could he have been otherwise described? Yes, durable.

What sort of gleanings from the FBI files did the aging but durable Hoover offer President Johnson? Juicy.

For which Johnson had what kind of appetite? Voracious.

Actress Sarah Miles was given a bash in a Madrid night club. What kind of bash and what kind of night club? Lavish and swank.

The annual increase in family budgets that would be brought on by President Ford's energy proposals was, according to one estimate, what? Whopping.

If a soldier is old, what else is he likely to be? Grizzled.

So goes *Time,* whopping and not ungrizzled itself, and still devoted to bbl. for barrel, bu. for bushel, and gal. for gallon. Roll out the bbl., don't hide your light under a bu., and a,b,c,d,e,f,g,h,i got a gallon in Kalamazoo.

Now that we know what *Time* can do, we are better able to judge what we can do ourselves. You will remember that we left the rangy Texan, the bluff head of Navy matériel, and the former Greek and Peruvian strongmen on a sprawling game reserve preparing to go on safari and having just learned that reservations for an ailing chief of state had been canceled and that if Daniel P. Moynihan did not exist he would have to be invented. Since then, sitting before a crackling log fire while Christmas slipped quietly into Bethlehem under the wary eye of Israeli guards, they have been discussing who else was going on the safari. The former Peruvian strongman spoke first:

"Listen," Velasco said, "is there any chance that we will see beetle-browed and pantalooned Kurdish leader Mulla Mustapha Barzani?"

"None," the Texan said. "He has slipped across the Iraqi border into Iran."

"Who told you?"

"Kurdish sources."

"Well placed?"

"It goes without saying."

Velasco persisted. "What about black-robed bearded prelate-president Archbishop Makarios, who once fled his island nation?"

"He won't be here either."

"How do you know?"

"Greek Cypriot sources."

"Familiar with his movements and in a position to know?"

"What do you think?"

"Piebald Robert Mardian of Watergate fame?"

"No."

"Pipe-smoking Harold Wilson?"

"I don't believe he can get away."

"But he no longer heads the deficit-ridden British government."

"True, but Britain is strike-plagued."

"What about the bewigged Speaker of the House of Commons?"

"Same problem."

"The steely-eyed Georgia peanut farmer, Jimmy Carter?"

"Ironing out differences."

"Crusty old George Meany?"

"Busy with a list of bread-and-butter Democratic liberals he would like to take to the woodshed."

"Why?"

"Because they broke with him on the all-important trade bill."

"Crusty sixty-five-year-old Christian President Suleiman Franjieh of Lebanon?"

"My understanding is no crusts of any description."

"The ambitious but sorely troubled Shah of Iran?"

"Dealing with his once burgeoning oil revenues."

"Short, blunt Teng Hsiao-p'ing?"

"Is he the same as tough, pragmatic Teng Hsiao-p'ing?"

"I believe so."

"Purged by his powerful enemies."

"On what charge?"

"Peddling sinister revisionist trash, and stirring the right-deviationist wind."

"What about a straight-talking foreign minister? The country doesn't matter."

"At the moment there aren't any."

"This is a damn dull safari," said the bluff Kidd.

"It'll perk up. It's only a matter of time," the Texan said. "Politically potent Italian Communist Party chief Enrico Berlinguer is coming."

"The spare Sardinian?"

"That's right."

"What's keeping him?"

"Maybe he ran into a papal motorcade," Velasco said.

"I doubt it," the Texan said. "The more likely explanation is that, as a spare Sardinian, he is much in demand for Sardinian dinner parties and has had trouble breaking away."

Kidd and Velasco stared out the window.

"I've never seen a military formation like it before," the Peruvian said, "if it is a military formation. One group is marching in the usual way, but the other seems to be falling over to the side."

The Texan, all business, went to the telephone and dialed the operator. "Hello," he said, "I'm a rangy Texan and a long way from home, where I am socially prominent. Get me an informed neutral source."

There was a pause, and then the Texan explained what they had seen. There was another pause, after which he said, "I understand," hung up, and turned to the others. "Perfectly simple, once you realize what it is. One left-leaning delegation and one crack regiment, arriving together to provide a façade of unity in this strife-torn continent."*

Velasco spoke. "That's how you know so much," he said to the Texan. "Sources."

"That's right."

"Have you ever met a neutral source?" Kidd asked.

"Only once."

"What was he like?"

"There wasn't time to find out," the Texan said. "He was a prestigious but self-effacing scholar, as many sources are, and he effaced himself before my eyes."

The former Greek strongman intervened. "I'm surprised that you did not recognize a left-leaning delegation on your own," he said. "Had you never seen one before?"

"Never," the Texan said. "Individuals, yes, but not delegations. And the left-leaning individuals I saw were otherwise perfectly ordinary. I'd like," he went on pensively, "to see some queer, soft, left-leaning eggheads who went to Harvard. Hard-driving, tenacious Woodward and Bernstein established their existence in *The Final Days*. Of course, they are exceptional reporters who know where to look when the rest of us don't."

---

* A reader suggested to me that politicians, journalists, and others who lean left may do so because of a faulty metatarsal arch. It was a stunning insight.

# Ize Front

In January 1976, before any of the presidential primaries, Howard "Bo" Callaway, chairman of President Ford's campaign committee, said, "The White House is so concerned about perceptions of a politicized White House that the President and those around him just totally unpoliticized the White House." After a number of Bo peeps of this kind, the President semirepoliticized the White House by bringing in Rogers Morton as a political counselor. Later, Callaway was put out to pasture, or pasturized.

The chairman of the Democratic National Committee, Robert Strauss, did not speak of unpoliticizing anything, but these were only healthy political differences, normal in a two-party system. In a discussion of who should have access to the Democratic convention floor, Strauss announced, "We're not going to depoliticize a political convention."

Toujours la politicizesse.

At a meeting of intellectuals to discuss UNESCO's attitude

toward Israel, Professor Seymour Martin Lipset of Stanford University said that the problem was "the politicalization of UNESCO."

Toujours la politicalizesse.

To ize a word is one thing. To wise it is another. Senator Birch Bayh of Indiana, campaigning for the Democratic nomination for President in October 1975—possibly on the theory that the early Birch catches the worm, which in this case it didn't—put forward the notion that a President can help the economy by sounding cheerful. One of our troubles, he said, was that "energywise, economywise and environmentalwise, we have become obsessed with the problems."

Affecting cheerfulness is not a notion with a history that commends it. During the Great Depression, prosperity spent an unconscionably long time just around the corner, and although Franklin Roosevelt's "We have nothing to fear but fear itself" has become a staple of television programs around inauguration time, the Depression was not beaten until the beginning of the Second World War. I can remember being panhandled when I was a boy in New York in the early 1930s and seeing the "Hooverville" huts of the poor and homeless along the banks of the Hudson. Happy talk did not help then any more than it helped Bayh.

If he were President, Bayh said in that same speech, and Federal Reserve Chairman Arthur Burns held back recovery by keeping money tight, "I'd create a structure to do an end run around him." Burns might of course have chosen to do a little running endwise himself, possibly tackling the structure before it got past the line of scrimmage. Moreover, if the other members of the Federal Reserve Board, joined by Federal Reserve bank presidents across the country, were to group themselves around Burns wedgewise, what could the structure—probably ad hoc, anyway, and rickety—have done?

Because Bayh abandoned his campaign for the nomination, we will never know the answer to that, though I would be inclined to put my money on Burns. Structures are nothing these days in Washington, where it is restructuring that counts. I am less in the dark about why Bayh tacked that wise onto energy, economy and environmental (it should have been environment) instead of saying, "We have become obsessed with the problems of energy, the economy and the environment," which is the same length syllablewise and more direct. Those who use wise as a suffix are convinced that they are saving time, because they are using one word instead of two. The program notes for a concert by the Chamber Music Society of Lincoln Center in New York had this: "Dvořák was a late bloomer, compositionwise."

If Dvořák was a late bloomer anythingwise, it was composerwise, but it is a small point.

"Been up to much lately, Antonin, compositionwise?"

"Quartetwise, it hasn't been bad, but symphonywise it's slow, and operawise . . ." His voice trails off. "I'm low," he says, "selfconfidencewise."

The misconception that time is being saved accounts for a wise to the word. The ize to the word comes about for another reason, which is that ize is thought to have a businesslike ring or, which in some cases is just as good, to sound technical. The *Wall Street Journal* reporter who covered Bayh's campaign in Boston spoke of the Democrats as "a factionalized party." No time was saved, since he could have said factional or, better still, factious. But he must have thought that factionalized carried more authority, which explains its appeal. What those who use ize overlook is that it is usually unnecessary, and always dull—it is a leaden syllable —and that it imposes monotony on the language by making so many words sound the same.

Not many can resist the temptation to ize. The *New York Times* said that a politician who went from agent to advisernegotiator for Mayor Abraham Beame had metamorphosized. It worked out fairly well but was a mixed metamorphosis. An adviser to Governor Hugh Carey of New York complained that members of the state legislature did not understand the urgency of New York's financial problems and so carried on as before. Said he, "They overstrategize themselves."

That over was significant. What is wanted in New York is the right amount of strategizing. A state senator sent me a copy of a proposal by an advertising company that wanted the $135,000 state contract for letting people know—"our objective is to generate measurable response"—about food stamps. After recommending radio announcements "because they offer access to the broadcast medium," meaning that if you put your announcements on radio they will be on radio, the company promised: "We will also strategize with the client on ways to optimize usage of the spots by broadcast management." The company got the contract. For linking strategize and optimize—somebody must have conceptualized this—it deserved to.

The Department of Public Instruction of the state of Iowa, conducting a survey of job prospects for those without a bachelor's degree, asked cooperating businesses to maximize the accuracy and validity of information supplied by keeping it as localized as possible. If they did, then the need for vocational training could be prioritized. Social and behavioral scientists never look back. Ize front.

I have been told that a television news broadcaster in Alabama announced that a deputy sheriff, killed in the line of duty, would be funeralized the following day, and there is, unfortunately, no reason to doubt it. United Press International, in a story about the Kennedy political tradition, remembered an occasion when John Kennedy prophecized. The Reverend Allison Cheek, one of the first women ordained in the Episcopal Church, said after celebrating communion, "I will not let the church inferiorize me again." Some believe that in the last analysis we are all humble, or inferiorized, servants of the Lord, but that covers everybody and takes away the sting. In other circumstances being inferiorized is no fun. I was covering the Turkish elections in 1957, relying on interpreters, as everyone else was. Then the BBC sent in a correspondent who spoke Turkish. It seemed to the rest of us that the BBC was hitting below the belt, but we were indubitably inferiorized. President Roy Amara of the Institute for the Future, an institute for the future in Menlo Park, California, prophecized not long ago, "Most of the influences on us today are rigidized for the next five years, and on a current momentum course that is irreversible." Five years carry the current momentum course to the point of no return, where it sees what the fates have in store if it continues. It reverses.

There is no limit to the bountiful imagination with which Americans ize. Sometimes I seem to hear thousands of voices raised in song:

> I fell in love with you
> First time I looked into
> Them there ize.

Americans annualize weekly and monthly costs and put out form letters that are personalized. Vulnerabilized to disease or traumatized by injury, they may be hospitalized. Because of the 1960s and 1970s, some of them have been cynicized and some radicalized. They privatize their houses with window shades and accessorize their spacious master bedrooms with oil paintings. As it happens, when the opportunity arose recently to accessorize my own spacious master bedroom with oil paintings, I could not seize it because I was making beautiful happen to my window treatments with Levolor Riviera blinds from Levolor Lorentzen, Inc., of Hoboken, New Jersey. Some days in New York, I wish I could make clean happen to my window treatments.

The publicity director of a publishing house received this letter from the assistant secretary of a large insurance company:

"Dear Mrs. C._____:

"We have finalized the structure of the program for our meetings in 1976, and unfortunately, the decision has been made not to utilize the services of an outside speaker. The decision on this was by no means unanimous, but by those whose final decision prevails. Perhaps sometime in the future we shall be able to put to use your services."

I knew what Mrs. C.'s feelings must have been. Many NBC program structures over the years have been finalized without putting to use my services. This sort of treatment is not without purpose. A British business slogan summed it up: Treat 'em mean and keep 'em keen.

Those in the government and academic world ize furiously. An art critic wondered what would happen to photography as a result of its museumization. The State Department has promised to utilize and vitalize ongoing machinery in dealing with the environment. A candidate for the Park Commission in Framingham, Massachusetts, offered analization of the park department's participation records. He was elected, but if the offer of analization was the reason, it would be interesting to know what the voters thought they were voting for. Maybe they could be psychoanalized.

During the 1974 campaign President Ford, verbalizing cuff-offwise at the airport in Greensboro, North Carolina, told the Republicans gathered there, some of them hard-nosed professionals, "Really, I look in your eyes and I plead with your hearts, and I beg with your mind, that you maximize your efforts." Maximize your efforts. A stirring call to arms.

It is often assumed that hardness of nose means that the owner of the nose is on the political right, or conservatized. It is not an infallible sign. C. L. Sulzberger of the *New York Times,* a connoisseur in such matters, gazed upon Helmut Schmidt, the Chancellor of West Germany, and declared him hard-nosed. A few weeks later Craig Whitney, chief of the Bonn bureau of the *Times,* examined Schmidt's nose and confirmed Sulzberger's finding. What neither appreciated is that a hard nose may help to keep the head level and sometimes above water. Complications arise not from a nose's obduracy—a hard nose turneth away wrath—but from its going where it is not wanted. Such a nose is not sensitized.

I once had a brief hope of being thought hard-nosed. One rainy day in Washington in 1946, I was at the airport covering President Truman's return from a trip, and another reporter mistook me for a Secret Service agent. I said nothing and concentrated on looking alert and rugged of nose. The hope faded when a real Secret Service agent told us, me included, to move back. My nose, which responds to flattery, wanted to continue the masquerade, but I knew that my hard-nosed days were over and that nothing lay ahead but being a two-fisted, shirt-sleeved newsman with a tough exterior concealing a heart as big as all outdoors.

An economist has pointed out to me a study (not his) in which the following appears:

"The definition of net wage rate in equation (2) suggests that wage-rate changes are best parameterized by changes in u." This is the first parameterized that has come to my attention. The study is dated October 1974. O Pioneers!

What is u? I do not know. I can tell u that the same study speaks of "an estimate which suffers from truncation bias." On a hunch, truncation bias means too small, pint-s, if I may say so, ized. A strange new language is emerging from the field in which this study was made. English is being econometricized. It is not for the better. Here is a passage from the study "Tax Effects on Job Search, Training, and Work Effort," by Jonathan R. Kesselman, published by the Institute for Research on Poverty at the University of Wisconsin:

*"Basic Properties of the Model*
"The assumed form of utility converts the problem to a two-stage maximization. For any given amount of leisure consumed, the worker wishes to choose the *income*-maximizing combination of search and work times. This determines his budget constraint in income-leisure space. Subject to this constraint, the worker chooses the *utility*-maximizing bundle of income and leisure.

"The income-maximizing choice of search time for any given leisure time is determined:

$$\delta Y/\delta S = 0 \longleftrightarrow HvW' - W = 0 .$$

"We call this the optimality condition for job-search. Let us interpret this condition under laissez faire (or any program other than a wage subsidy):

$$W(S) = HW' \text{ with } u = 0 .$$

"A worker is spending the optimal time on search when a marginal hour will earn him the same amount at work, $W(S)$, as at search, $HW'$. Because v enters both sides of the equality, its value does not affect the result. Search optimality is not dependent on the marginal utilities, owing to the assumed utility form (6). The second-order condition for (7) to be a maximum rather than a minimum solution is:

$$\delta^2 Y/\delta S^2 < 0 \longleftrightarrow HW'' - 2W' < 0 .$$

"Before proceeding to the second stage of the maximization, we examine two properties of the income-maximizing budget constraint. The slope is readily established."

Since, as Kesselman says, the slope is readily established, it need not detain us. We move ahead to the point at which, Kesselman says, we may "conventionally assume the utility function to be twice differentiable and concave:

$$C = W^2 U_{YY} - 2WU_{YL} + U_{LL} < 0 .$$

"We shall later state the stronger second-order condition needed for an internal tangency in the presence of the convex budget constraint. Let us designate income the numeraire good. Then the first-order condition for the worker's utility-maximum will be:

$$U_Y = U_L/W .$$

"This is the familiar first-order condition of the standard labor-supply model."

It does have a certain familiarity about it. It is living beyond your numeraire good that is the problem.

A historian, Richard Morris of Columbia University, has told other historians that during the American Revolution the Tories were fifth columnists and that they should not now be heroized. I was not aware of any mad rush to heroize the Tories for the Bicentennial, but hasty izing does sometimes have to be undone, or neutralized. Hugh M. Bowen, associate professor of applied psychology at Stevens Institute of Technology in Hoboken, New Jersey, has pointed out that, in Britain, prostitution has been de-illegalized. There is already a movement in the United States to have marijuana decriminalized.

Obviously, if ize were avoided in the first place, no one would have to de. It may be stated as a rule: ize before de. Africa, for example, could not have gone through decolonization if it had not been colonized first. Also, ize before re. "Since 1967," an Israeli journalist told the *New Yorker,* "we have been reghettoized." And fy before de. When the French Communist Party became openly less dependent on Moscow, a French analyst explained, "It is de-Russifying itself, but not de-Stalinizing." When the Viking I space robot landed on Mars in July 1976, John Leonard of the *New York Times* wrote about the prospects for demythifying the planet. They were bright. Demythifie on you, John Leonard. But there are exceptions to the rule, especially where covert activities are concerned. Governments are ripest for destabilizing when they have not been stabilized to begin with. Thus the CIA destabilized the Allende government in Chile, and the leader of the Portuguese Communists, of all people, saucily complained that reactionary forces were trying to destabilize Portuguese politics. This was prestabilization destabilization, de taking place before our very ize.

The terms were unknown to me at the time, but I went through heroization and deheroization in short order in 1941, just after I went to work in the International News Service bureau in Washington, and years before my—the Canadians are no slouches at izing; this is the *Toronto Globe and Mail's* word—televisionization. I was in the Senate press gallery, much impressed with everything, including myself for being there, when Senator John Overton of Louisiana, an ally of Governor Huey Long, rose to attack the columnist Thomas Stokes. Stokes had written an exposé of the misuse of federal money by the Long machine, and had received a Pulitzer, or, as Overton prophetically put it, had been Pulitzerized. He repeated the word a number of times with deep sarcasm. He waved his arms and his face grew red. He seemed dangerously angry.

Soon after Overton finished, I left the gallery and entered one of the elevators reserved for Senators and the press. Stokes was in the car also. One floor down, Overton got in. The car was small, and Overton and Stokes were cheek (Overton's) by (Stokes's) jowl. I saw myself getting a scoop as Overton flung himself frenziedly on Stokes, and I—more than a reporter, a hero—pulled them apart.

"Hello, Tom," said Overton.

"Hiya, Senator," said Stokes.

"Goodbye, scoop," said Newman to himself. "Goodbye, hero."

I was also deheroized with great dispatch when I returned to the United Press Washington bureau near the end of 1945. I made the rounds, saying hello to those who had stayed on through the war, and I was exceedingly glad when the night-side editor, known to be dour and demanding, welcomed me with great warmth. I was congratulating myself on the reputation I had obviously made in the bureau three and a half years before, when the night editor spoke again. "Now," he said, "at last we can get rid of some of those damned women."

Rapid heroization and deheroization is my lot. In the spring of 1976, George Washington High School, in New York City, decided that it would have a Hall of Fame of graduates and would hold a dinner to celebrate it. The actresses Jean Arthur and Paulette Goddard were among those chosen, and Henry Kissinger, and Alan Greenspan, Harold Robbins, the novelist, and Senator Jacob Javits, and the baseball player Rod Carew. So was I. I sent in my check for the dinner. It came back. Enough members of the Hall of Fame were willing to attend and be goggled at, but other alumni, not famous, who would have had to do the goggling, no.

Prolonged observation—by me, not of me—has led me to the conclusion that the most widespread izing now going on among Americans is optimizing. Americans are insisting on freedom to optimize, and this may become an inalienable right. It is being popularized.

I learned from a report by the Central and Southern Florida Flood Control District that optimization techniques play a large part in water resources management. These techniques require, among other things, optimization models, conceptual visualization, parametric analysis, inputs, overall methodologies, the inclu-

sion of all viable pathways in the system evaluation schemes, statistical deterministic models, statistical probabilistic models, and,
of course, minimization and maximization, the Damon and Pythias
of our time.

Congress optimizes, as indeed, since it speaks for the American people, it should. A House-Senate conference committee considering an oil bill reported that the bill was designed to optimize
production from domestic properties. This was to be done through
a pricing system intended to give the President "a substantial
measure of administrative flexibility to craft the price regulatory
mechanism in a manner designed to optimize production from domestic properties subject to a statutory parameter requiring the
regulatory pattern to prevent prices from exceeding a maximum
weighted average." Here is a standard to which all free men will
repair.

Not all congressional language is of this kind, though the
amount is unquestionably increasing. My mind goes back to the
late 1940s and the English used by Ab Herman, administrative assistant to Senator H. Alexander Smith of New Jersey. Herman
would hand a press release to another staff member with the instruction, "Give it the backdrop," meaning "Put in the background. Put it in context." Another instruction was "Bulletproof
it," meaning take out any mistakes. This admirable brevity may
have been a product of his days as a professional baseball player
before good velocity took over.*

It almost seems that everybody optimizes. William D. Lawson,
class of 1949, running for the Cornell University Board of
Trustees, thought that he deserved support because, he wrote, one
of his principal interests in the business world (he was assistant
general manager of Du Pont's fabrics and finishes department) was
long-range versus short-range optimization. He thought, Mr. Lawson wrote, that this was probably the most difficult problem that
faced a university, partly because the educational needs for a satisfying and contributing life tended to cyclize. Mr. Lawson was not

---

* See page 86.

elected and had to look for a satisfying and contributing life elsewhere.

The Engineering Division of the Travelers Insurance Companies of Hartford, Connecticut, optimized in a pamphlet on product quality and safety: "The question arises, 'If one has optimized a stable design and a well-directed manufacturing operation, why is a quality control program necessary?' The primary answer is *people*. Since no perfect human being exists at this time, errors can and do contaminate the manufacturing cycle. To minimize these errors, the total manufacturing cycle must be policed to assure product/design integrity." The Travelers missed a significant point. It said that people cause errors, even with a well-directed manufacturing operation and optimized stable design. That is precisely why no perfect human being exists at this time. Because of the difficulty of policing the total manufacturing cycle, which remains stubbornly privatized, none is likely to any time soon.

Many foreigners have written that the American character has been shaped by the fact that we are still a young country, rich in ideals and resources, and with the frontier only recently closed. This explains why so few Americans pessimize. However, I do not want to exaggerate this aspect of the American character. Many of those who do not pessimize nonetheless nonoptimize, so that the absence of pessimizational activity does not necessarily imply the presence of optimizational activity.

Non, which is becoming as popular at the beginning of words as ize is at the end, has many uses. It can be vaguely neutral. After President Ford went to China a committee of the National Press Club declared that his press secretary, Ron Nessen, had given "a disastrous non-performance." Said the committee: "Nessen lunged to his nadir." A nadir is a nonzenith. Strictly speaking, it is an anti-zenith. Without the disastrous and the nadir, non-performance might almost have been taken as noncommittal.

However, non may also be discriminatory and pejorative, as in the case of those who are nonsmokers, nondrivers, and nonwhite. The other identity dominates—smoking, driving, and being white are the affirmative acts, and they define the relation. Being non means being classified according to what you do not do and are not. In the United States, not driving a car is roughly equivalent to not existing, and people who do not drive find that they often have trouble paying by check because they cannot produce a driver's license. A few states issue nondriver identification cards, and in one state a legislator proposed a non-driver's license. The proposal may have been inspired by generosity of spirit, though it sounded as if those who did not drive would need licenses to be permitted not to. This may be coming.

There is a movement among those encouraging the teaching of Indian languages and literature—at South Dakota State University, for example—to refer to Indians as Native Americans and to other Americans as non-Native Americans. This is a narrow view of nativity, and would make people nonnatives of the country in which they were born. Perhaps they could be given resident aliens' visas.

Politically, non may imply a favorable judgment. Americans for Democratic Action refers to certain Senators and Representatives as non-Southern Democrats, though Southern Democrats are not known to the ADA as non-Northern Democrats. Being non-Southern is the desired characteristic. During the oil embargo in 1974, being non-Arab was a considerable recommendation in itself.

Sometimes non is used to be reassuring. Nonlethal gas is thought by those who use it in police and military actions to be almost benevolent. Walt Disney's amusement parks, according to a writer in *Signature,* offer nonperilous adventure. Night clubs recruiting dancers will specify nontopless so that prospective employees will know that they need not go about half-naked. Though non-Southern means Northern, nontopless does not mean bottomless. A night club offering that kind of dancing, perhaps called the Bottomless Pit, would probably state it more plainly. Its dancers would go about dressed to the nons. Non may also be used evasively, as in the case of the liquid that goes into tea and coffee and is called aerated nondairy creamer. One blanches to think what aerated nondairy creamer would be called on the basis of what it is rather than what—dairy cream—it is not.

I mentioned earlier the State Department's promise to utilize and vitalize ongoing machinery. The stated purpose was to strengthen an ever broadening dialogue on the environment. Ever broadening dialogues, which go from the particular to the general to the global to the cosmic and then to horizons not yet dreamed of, are intended to enable nations to deal with each other on the basis of what Secretary of State Kissinger called non-belligerency, including, he specified, the non-use of force. Each side monitors the other closely to be sure that force is what it is nonusing and— Kissinger again—pursues energetically all signs of noncompliance. If neither side has reason to say to the other, "You noncomplied," or if one does noncomply but gets away with saying that it will nonrecur, both may find themselves on what Senator Henry Jackson, in the kind of language that helped to end his campaign for the Democratic presidential nomination, called a nonadversary basis.* They may also find themselves, if the dialogue has not ceased to broaden, non compos mentis.

A nonmember is as different as different can be from a nonchairman member. A nonchairman member is a member. He is simply not the chairman. This may be easily grasped in the following *New York Times* dispatch:

"Albany, April 6—Governor Carey's office is actively considering† withdrawing the nomination of Herman Schwartz as chairman of the Commission of Correction and renominating him as one of the two nonchairman members of the prison watchdog agency."

A nonmember is neither a chairman nor a member, and would not be expected to show up for meetings at all. In fact, nonmembers should be careful about the meetings they do go to. Rabbi Arthur Hertzberg, president of the American Jewish Congress,

---

* Someone may have written this phrase for Jackson under a non de plume.

† To be distinguished from inactively considering.

complained because remarks he made at a meeting in Israel were picked up and reported. "I took it," he said, "to be a nonpublic meeting."

Nonmembers should not be confused with, for example, non-minority group members. A nonminority group member is a non-member of a minority group but a member of a nonminority—formerly called a majority—group. To remain a nonmember, it is useful to be a noncommunist and noncontroversial. This helps the nomination of a nonmember to get through. The time may be coming when, to retain one's position as a nonmember, it will be best not to be a nonlawyer. This is because Chief Justice Warren Burger has proposed that nonlawyers be appointed to small-claims courts in place of judges, I presume after they have spent some years in non-law school. Burger's idea has been to this point what the British call a nonstarter. Burger might have been wiser to submit the idea first to a nonprofit, nongovernmental research or-ganization for analysis—nonpartisan, of course—before making it nonprivate.

To be a nonmember, it helps to be also a nonpolitician who is a noncandidate for public office. There are, as always, exceptions. In 1976, Hubert Humphrey remained a noncandidate against heavy odds. Equally, being a nonpolitician is not an infallible guarantee of retention of nonmember status. In early 1976 the New York Times reported that Daniel Patrick Moynihan, "who enjoys an image as a nonpolitician," might run for the Senate. The Times added that Democrats who definitely did want to run "for the most part cultivated an antipolitics image." This could have discouraged Moynihan, for the others, being anti to his non, were more negatively charged against politics than he was. None of this made much sense to me. Since the antipolitician and the nonpolitician would lose anti and non status, respectively, imme-diately upon election, their appeal was fleeting. Nor was it sug-gested that if Moynihan went to the Senate his place at Harvard should be taken by a nonscholar, though nonscholars are occa-sionally invited to lecture at universities to let in a breath of nonstale air. Nonetheless, a candidate who was in favor of politics, which might seem logical for someone seeking political office, evidently stood no chance at all. He would offend the nonvoters.

When political news is heavy, NBC likes to have as many employees on hand as possible. This is why an NBC memorandum once described the news assignment desk as being in a nonvacation, full-staff configuration. If you do intend to take a nonvacation, your place of work is the best place to do it. Configuratively speaking.

The appeal of non is nondifferent from the appeal of ize. It sounds technical, which is why doctors often speak of nonemergency rather than elective surgery. Beyond that, non suggests not that something is being done but that something is not, which perhaps makes it easier to swallow. The Superior, Wisconsin, *Telegram* quoted Chancellor Karl Meyer of the Superior campus of the University of Wisconsin on his attempt to limit reductions in the university budget. If the cuts were smaller, the *Telegram* reported Meyer as saying, it might be possible to save the jobs of some who "would otherwise be non-retained." If not, Meyer would be the old family nonretainer.

Any teachers on the Superior campus who have been nonretained may be able to find jobs in New York State with the Project on Noncollegiate-Sponsored Instruction. The Project is designed to obtain college credits for those who have taken courses from corporations, volunteer groups, state agencies, and other organizations and institutions classified as—need I say?—nonacademic.

Although non can sound neutral and even faintly reassuring, as in nontopless and nonlethal, de cannot. De is almost brutal. It means that something is being removed, or got rid of, or abandoned. The hunger to use de is almost as great as the hunger to use ize and non. When Sam Jaffe was a television news correspondent he also worked undercover for the FBI. Jaffe covered for CBS the trial in Moscow of Francis Gary Powers, the U–2 pilot shot down in 1960, and when he returned to the United States, Jaffe said, he was debriefed by agents of the FBI. When Richard Nixon went to China in February 1976, Secretary of State Kissinger said that details of the debriefing would be decided on Nixon's return.

In both cases there was a misunderstanding. If debrief means anything, it means to withdraw instructions, usually those given to a lawyer, and it is a thoroughly unnecessary term. The FBI was not debriefing Jaffe, and the State Department was not debriefing Nixon. Jaffe and Nixon were the ones who had the experiences and were giving the summaries. They were doing the briefing. The FBI and the State Department were asking questions, at most. But government people who think of themselves as debriefers do not look at things that way. For them the active role in the transaction is theirs. The others are merely debriefees. Hardly has their man deplaned—which is another misnomer; the plane is being cleared of people, not the other way around—than they are all over him, debriefcases at the ready, to find out what he knows.

Debriefing also may follow quickly on deshipping, detraining, or decarring, and sometimes word will be passed that the debriefee has been wrongly classified. Debriefing is intended for friends. The harsher process of deprogramming is substituted for non-friends and friends who have been indoctrinated by nonfriendly forces. In particularly stubborn cases deprogramming is accompanied by threats that those not yielding up their programs fast enough will be defunded. There is a distinct difference here from debriefing, for those who are defunded must first have been funded (Funded in 1876. A Hundred Years of Service). They will also be threatened with being delisted, that is, taken off lists they would like to be on,* and in some countries they may be threatened with captivity in rooms that have been delamped, which is not the same as being delighted and carries an implied threat that the captives may shortly become defunct. They realize that continuing to hold

---

* Project Equality, a religious group that devotes itself to equal employment opportunity, may delist companies from its *Buyers Guide* after conducting or not being allowed to conduct "validation reviews of selected facility implementation." Members of Project Equality are then informed of the companies' "delisted status." I've got, KoKo might have sung, a little delist.

out in a defunded condition, when they don't have a fund in the
world, will only generate diseconomies for them. This is a disin-
centive to continued defiance. Debriefed, deprogrammed, and de-
jected, they desist.

The supreme comment on de came from Harry W. Hiscock, of
Rochester, New York, a private in the Marine Corps who was
shot in the hand as part of "hazing" by a drill instructor at Parris
Island, South Carolina. "They talk about motivation around
here," the private said. "Well, ever since what happened, I've felt
very de-motivated."

The private was assigned to a medical rehabilitation platoon
whose doctors hoped that the second knuckle and other parts of
his hand could be rebuilt, and, one supposes, his motivation with
them. They could not be, and Hiscock was given a disability pen-
sion. The Marines talk a great deal about motivation. Private
Lynn McClure, of Lufkin, Texas, twenty years old and said to be
mentally retarded, died of brain damage three months after being
beaten with "pugil sticks." Pugil sticks are poles tipped with pad-
ding that are used in bayonet training. According to other recruits
who took part, when McClure did not want to fight and said that he
was injured the drill sergeants ordered the others to beat him. One
of those who did the beating told the *Los Angeles Times:* "Just to
beat on this guy gave us the feeling that the drill instructor liked
this and that we were really showing motivation."

McClure was in the "incentive section" of the "motivation platoon." It cannot be argued that if the Marines did not speak of
motivation McClure would be alive. But motivation is one of those
fashionable words that smack of psychology and pedagogy. It en-
ables those who use it to conceal from themselves what those they
are motivating are being motivated to do. It camouflages reality.
We are all safer when language is specific. It improves our chances
of knowing what is going on.

A faculty member at a university I had better not name received a memorandum from a high administrative officer of the
institution: "Having prioritized available funding, your request for
staff-support facilities cannot be actuated at present. Student

throughput* indicators show marked declining motivational values in subsequent enrollment periods in elective liberal arts choices." My correspondent thought that meant his request had been turned down.

I have written of certain syllables that mean a great deal to people in government and the academic world—ize, de, dis, ive, re, fy. Ful is another. To say that something was impactful rather than that it had an effect sounds official. News people like it too. It makes *them* sound official. A correspondent for the Public Broadcasting Service asked the head of an agency whether the resignation of a colleague would be majorly impactful on the agency's work. The PBS correspondent should have been deprogrammed at once but wasn't.

I have been told of an executive in an advertising agency who wrote to a client: "This will enable us to direct the most maximally impactful advertising toward the small and medium size dog owner." And the least maximally impactful toward the large size dog owner.

Ive has many applications also. The chairman of President Ford's election campaign, Rogers Morton, said that a Cabinet "ought to be made up of competent people who are qualified to do the job but who are totally supportive of the President." A doubtful thesis, as Vietnam and Watergate demonstrated, but doubtful or not, Morton could have said "who support the President." Perhaps "totally supportive of" is thought to denote a higher level of loyalty, but that is not the reason for using it. It has a quality much loved in Washington. It is ponderous. "The issues," an expert has proclaimed, "are promotive of apathy." So are words like promotive and endorsive.†

To combine dis and ive is especially esteemed. The lieutenant

---

* The meaning of throughput here is obscure. It may refer to students' intentions. A State Department definition of throughput— jazzily spelled thruput—may be found on page 96.

† Benjamin DeMott, reviewing a novel by Alan Lelchuk in the *Atlantic,* wrote, "Mr. Lelchuk is never endorsive of fatuity." Endorsements of fatuity, except in election years, are rare.

governor of New York, Mary Anne Krupsak, said that opponents of the Equal Rights Amendment ran "the most distortive political campaign ever to unfold." The Librarian of Congress, Daniel Boorstin, in an address to the Association of American Publishers, spoke of "the displacive fallacy." I do not know what Boorstin meant, but it is clear that dis and ive unite as smoothly as de and ize, although more often than not de ize have it.

Ive is particularly in vogue with economists. Democrats on the Joint Congressional Economic Committee have sometimes called for more stimulative fiscal and monetary policies, with the Republicans replying that economic recovery required that Congress refrain from further stimulative measures. In January 1976 the Council of Economic Advisers, though recommending a deceleration in the growth of federal spending and concerned about renewed imbalances and sectoral distortions, argued that some stimulative measures were needed so that the country could return to high levels of resource utilization.

There is not a more depressive word in existence than stimulative, unless it is disstimulative, which I have not yet seen but which cannot be far off. In the meantime, a writer for the *Montreal Star* has produced this: "Fiscal and monetary policy, it has now been shown, is not, by itself, enough to stimulate or disstimulate the economy."

These syllables—dis, ative, ization—sound learned. They are the stuff of reports. They turn any paper in which they appear into a document. Not the least of such syllables is ee, a syllable drawn from the French and with a long and honorable history, as in fiancée, devotee, and refugee, but seized upon by governments and academics to enable them to speak more stuffily and so with greater self-importance. People invited are now called invitees. I expect schoolchildren soon to be called educatees, and one to whom money is owed a debtee.

When Portugal's colonies became independent, thousands of people left them. They were refugees. That was not, however, their official designation. To the Portuguese government, which must have thought refugee old-fashioned, they were returnees. It is the fate of returnees to be among those most likely to be debriefed and to be made, willee nillee, debriefees. Sometimes, to become returnees they must first become escapees, a word government agencies use—misuse—to mean those who escape.

"To what do you attribute your escape?"

"I am a fast runnee."

If the question is phrased in a more up-to-date manner—"To what do you attribute your successful escape?"—the answer is the same.* In this country some debriefees have been detailees. Detailees are people the CIA details to other duties, meaning that they are slipped into other government agencies. When they get back they are expected to tell all:

"What are you doing, Empson?"

"Debriefing a detailee, sir."

"Why is it taking so long?"

"It's all the confounded detail, sir."

"Can't you speed things up?"

"I will ask the debriefee to be brief, sir."

It fell to me to speak at a luncheon in honor of those who in 1975 completed twenty-five years with NBC. They were called new quarter-century club honorees. There is a phrase to quicken the blood and spark the imagination. At that, the honorees could have been worse off. After appearing on the "Today" show one morning, two representatives of the Golf Hall of Fame, in Augusta, Georgia, generously gave Gene Shalit and me copies of the Golf Hall of Fame Diary. A little later, they sent us two more copies and a letter of apology because the originals had not included the names of the 1975 enshrinees. If needs must, it is better to be honored than enshrined. It is better to be a retiree than an enshrinee, though it may expose you to such pronouncements as this one from the Home Insurance Company of Boston: "This change does not apply to the spouse of a retiree or active employee already deceased."

Rather than enshrinees, protectees be, which is what a spokes-

---

* See page 164.

man for the Secret Service—how can you have a spokesman for a secret service?—made of President Ford and his family. Enshrinement sounds so (here I acknowledge my debt to Representative John Murphy of New York, who could not bear to call a final paragraph final) conclusionary.

Using excess syllables makes words longer. That is often the purpose; it is an attempt to impress, and it goes on all over the country. No region wants to be left out. In Washington the House committee deciding whether President Nixon should be impeached studied not evidence but evidentiary material. Ality and icity also extend and inflate. A recent university graduate wrote to the public relations department of a large corporation in Redwood City, California, "My purpose in writing you and applying for a position with your firm is ultimately a selfish one: I need a professional context in which to give a more mature, enlightened and constructive shape to my rhetoricality." He suggested "that you revolutionize your rhetoric to the point of giving greater credence to the multiplicity of language forms." His language form was one to which the company did not give credence, and he was not offered a professional context.

In New York the Chase Manhattan Bank closed a branch on Times Square not because it had lost money but because of continuing unprofitability. At a meeting of the board of directors of the Transit District of Orange County, California, at which one of the members spoke of "the growingness of the Transit District," the board considered a market plan containing this sentence: "A communication objective built around the concept of trialability has been developed. . . . If trialability is achieved, that, in itself, will contribute to the education of the population."

It is debatable whether education of the population should be in the hands of anyone who believes that trialability is a word, or of anyone who believes that growingness is. It is already in the hands of some who have strange ideas about such matters, among them Sheila Huff, research associate at Syracuse University; Albert Shanker, president of the United Federation of Teachers; and a group of teachers in and around Appleton, Wisconsin. Ms. Huff wrote for the May 1974 issue of the *Harvard Educational Review* an article called, "Credentialing by Tests or Degrees: Title VII of the Civil Rights Act and *Griggs* v. *Duke Power Company*." With this diploma, I thee credential. She passed the torch to Shanker, who wrote, "One of the major functions of the schools has been to act as a credentialing agency." The teachers in Wisconsin, out on strike, informationally leafleted other teachers about their grievances. Leafleting and credentialing may also go on among the religious. The *Anglican Digest*, reporting on the death of the bishop of Western North Carolina, noted that he had been consecrated in 1948 and priested in 1936. I wonder when he was postulanted and noviced. A Texas museum has announced juried exhibits. Pilots flying from London to New York will announce: "We have just overheaded Shannon." The trappings of office include, for some office trappers, a chauffeured limousine. Democrats accused other Democrats of wanting a brokered convention. Instead, they got a credentialed one. Said Frederic A. Bennett, assistant security director for the Democrats at Madison Square Garden, "To our knowledge, no one, absolutely no one, got into the Garden this week who was not properly credentialed." It was my sixth Democratic convention but the first at which I was among the credentialees. A laxative has proclaimed itself chocolated, which reminds me of the days of austerity in Britain after the Second World War, when some foods were so scarce that you might find yourself being served baconed scrambled egg, which apparently meant that the bacon had been swirled around the pan before the eggs were cooked much as Vermouth is swirled around the pitcher for an extra dry martini. A correspondent with an APO address told me about some people who came home and found their house ramshackled. They must have been gone a long time. During the Montreal Olympics, ABC Sports told us about horses in the equestrian competition that had not done much eventing, and about swimmers who medaled. I now expect athletes also to trophy, ribbon, and cup, champions to title, and professionals to purse.

One other syllable ought to be mentioned, for it may be joining non and someday may even displace it.* That syllable is un. The makers of Seven-Up use it, advertising the drink as the Uncola. Un has also been used by manufacturers of handbags who wanted to stop saying that their products were made of plastic or imitation leather or, in one case, genuine imitation simulated leather. Unleather, they called it, and it certainly was. This opens new possibilities—uncowhide, unfur, uncotton, and fire warnings telling us not to walk but to unrun to the nearest exit.† All things considered, it may be wise to note the location of the nearest exit now.

---

* I hope that I am not falling prey here to the displacive fallacy.

† Jesse Unruh, the California Democrat, may move on to new political triumphs.

# A Real Super Player
# with Good Compassion

A few years ago, after the relief pitcher Mike Marshall was traded to the Los Angeles Dodgers, he found himself rooming with another pitcher, Andy Messersmith, when the team traveled. The effect on Messersmith was profound. "I'm a better student of hitters since Mike joined us," said Messersmith. "My studiology of baseball is better." Marshall is a Ph.D. who worries more about facing variables during a game than about facing batters; probably the studiology he elicited from Messersmith was to be expected. Though this be madness, yet there's methodology in it. It is only part of a larger movement in which the language of sports grows more pretentious.

Sports are being overcome by the All-American urge, the urge to complicate. Much of the news on the sports pages these days has less to do with the games played than with the circumstances in which they are played, and under whose auspices, and with what guarantees, and with what ancillary income arrangements, and whether they will be played at all. Athletes are growing what in the military would be called administrative and logistic tails—lawyers, agents, advisers, publicity specialists, all of them experts in turning fame into money.

When contests do take place, they are less an end in themselves than a means by which the players go on to other things. The principal purpose of winning the figure-skating gold medal in the Olympics, so it appears, is to have a professional career. Mark Spitz's seven gold medals in swimming in the 1972 Olympics were worth a fortune, though Spitz as an entertainer—or, a more nebulous category, a personality—could barely stay afloat. Cogito, ergo swim. In the spring of 1976, Larry Csonka, who had jumped from the National Football to the World Football League, jumped back, the World etc. having globally failed. He signed with the New York Giants, and one reason he chose them, Csonka explained, was that the promotional—outside income—possibilities were greater in New York than anywhere else. In that same spring the Oakland A's traded outfielder Reggie Jackson to Baltimore. Jackson did not want to go because his outside interests were on the West Coast. So was a 1975 batting average of .253. How can a player with a .253 average have outside interests?

Obviously athletes should think about the future and should bargain, individually and collectively, for the best deal they can get. I hope that they are better protected than some of the celebrated athletes of the past, especially fighters, who sometimes found that more of them was owned by others than existed. There were cases in which 150 per cent of a fighter's contract was sold. Distribution of 150 per cent of the purse did not leave much for him.

Still, the almost endless haggling and legal dueling that have become standard are tiresome. Most sports stories now provide about as much entertainment and excitement as the briefs filed in railroad bankruptcy cases. A topheavy structure of complication, negotiation, and protocol is being reared on the competition that actually does take place and on the frequently modest talents of those competing. As a result the language of sports more and more resembles the language of politics and diplomacy—a new reciprocity, for politicians and political writers have traditionally borrowed from sports to show that they are not stuffy and that they have the common touch. An election year can hardly begin before somebody is designated the front runner, and there is talk of staying up in the pack, and this candidate makes a grandstand play, and that candidate picks his spots, and So-and-so has momentum but has only faced the second team* and it may be different when he goes one on one with Such-and-such on his home ground.

After Ronald Reagan beat President Ford in the Indiana primary, the Republican chairman in Michigan, William McLaughlin, pronounced the contest for the nomination "a real ball game." That made it a doubleheader, because Representative Morris Udall was at that same time pronouncing the Democratic contest a whole new ball game, and even predicting that he would be in the play-offs. It wasn't and he wasn't. Before the Pennsylvania primary Senator Henry Jackson said that it would be well to come first in the preferential voting there "but the name of the game is delegates." Soon thereafter the name eluded the Senator, going through to Jimmy Carter, who gathered it in on one hop, while remarking in Portland, Oregon, on May 19, "The name of the game is delegates," and Jackson was relegated to the bench.†

When the United States lent Britain $3,750,000,000 in 1946, a reporter at Secretary of the Treasury Fred Vinson's news conference told Vinson that he had been sitting in left field and had not heard Vinson's answers. "Well," said Vinson, a right-handed Secretary, "I'm a pull hitter." The military, too, borrow from sports. During the North African campaign in the Second World War, the British commander, General Sir Bernard Montgomery, assured his men that they would hit the German commander, Field

---

* On the night Jimmy Carter won the Illinois primary, I asked him whether it was not true that, with Hubert Humphrey and Edward Kennedy out, he was facing the Democrats' second team. He sidestepped and swung around me for an easy score.

† Sometimes rendered as regulated to the bench.

Marshal Erwin Rommel, for six. That is the cricket equivalent of a pronouncement by Harry Dent, Ford's Southern delegate co-ordinator, after the President visited Mississippi: "He knocked it over the fence." The temptation to borrow from sports overcomes judges, also. In Santa Fe, New Mexico, two prosecutors claimed the right to work with a county grand jury. "Neither of the two players," said Judge Edwin Felter, "shall decide which thereof shall carry the ball." Football huddle talk by a quarterback: "Whereas their left defensive end is consistently out of position, I shall now hear closing arguments against a quick opener off right tackle, and if none be forthcoming, I shall issue a writ of manda-mus for said play forthwith."

The results of this cultural borrowing are not always happy. James R. Dickenson of the *Washington Star* covered a news con-ference held by Vice President Nelson Rockefeller and reported: "Rockefeller leaned nonchalantly on the podium and made no effort to field the inevitable question. He just stood and let it go by him." Anybody leaning on a podium, which is a low dais of the kind orchestra conductors stand on, would not be in a position to field anything. He would not be standing. He might be doing a one-arm push-up. Politicians do sometimes lean nonchalantly on the party platform, but that is different. The platform is pleased to be noticed at all.

I assume that Rockefeller was leaning on a lectern while standing on a podium while making no effort to field the inevitable question, which was whether he would try for the Republican nomination if Ford did poorly in the early 1976 primaries and dropped out. Rockefeller, of course, had gone after the nomina-tion before—he "made a real good try on that one"—and had shown second effort. "He always gives a thousand per cent."

Now the traffic is flowing in the other direction. When Csonka —who, like all other players, including Rockefeller, is some kind of player—signed with the Giants, no details were announced except that he had signed a "multiyear" contract. That was instead of a uniyear contract for players in less demand. When Joe Frazier and George Foreman signed for their June 1976 multirounder, sportswriters were proud to attribute their information about the contract to "a highly placed boxing source." A boxing source bobs and weaves, feints with a left, and then throws a right that delivers the goods. A boxing judge, Harold Lederman, replying to a letter to a newspaper from the referee Barney Felix, wrote that Felix's words in reprehension of the sport were an unexpected animadversion that shocked him deeply. He felt strongly compelled to express his complete and utter incredulity. When I look at the language of sports, I often am myself.

Lederman's letter may have been ghost written by Howard Cosell, who speaks of teams in a poor field position situation, and of a back who will run unmolestedly down the field, thereby enabling his team to perpetrate a major upset, which may revivify the fans' interest or, if they are on the other side, lead them to give vent to their vocal discontent, rather as Muhammad Ali did before the George Foreman fight in Zaire, when he rendered himself, so Cosell told us, into a hoarse frenzy. During the Ali–Jimmy Young fight in April 1976, Cosell noted that Ali attemptedly delivered a number of punches. Young attemptedly blocked them. On another night, during half-time of a football game, Cosell announced, "I am variously bounded and circumscribed by Senator Edward Kennedy and John Denver." Kennedy was, geographically, on one side of him and Denver on the other.

Unfortunately, Cosell is not alone. Early in the 1975 professional football season, during a game between the New York Jets and the Kansas City Chiefs, Charlie Jones of NBC noticed Joe Namath raging about a call of offensive pass interference and announced that Namath was holding a détente with the officials. Actually, it was a démarche accompanied by an aide-mémoire, ending in a tour d'horizon. Luckily, the officials did not declare Namath persona non grata and ask for his recall.

On NBC, Jim Simpson described David Knight, a wide receiver for the New York Jets, as "a young man not of any specific speed and any specific size, who makes a living by knowing how to run the patterns." It is because Knight is of no specific size that, after he catches the ball, he is so hard to tackle. Simpson also told us, before a Miami-Baltimore game, that Miami was driving for its sixth consecutive play-off in a row. Many sports broadcasters now believe that consecutive is shorthand for consecutive in a row, just as eight straight wins seems incomplete to them alongside eight straight wins without a loss, and they would rather not take the easy way. All credit to them. All credit also to NBC, which told me one late summer day that college football had made its first full-fledged debut of the season, in a game in which one side beat the other closer than expected. And to CBS, which reported on what had to be the most westernmost football game played in the U.S. (It was in Hawaii.) Having to be most westernmost is a distinction and not to be spoken about in reprehension.

Sports broadcasters often have a shaky grip on grammar and on the connection between words and meaning. I learned one night from NBC that Dock Ellis, a pitcher formerly with the Pittsburgh Pirates, was "looking ahead to a low-profile image with the Yankees." A low-profile image is not unlike a poor field position situation and involves keeping an ear to the ground. From Brent Musberger of CBS, I learned during a game between the New York Jets and the Dallas Cowboys that "Tom Henderson found an opening and blocked Greg Gant's would-be kick." The would-be kick was disappointed at failing to fulfill its potential and promised to be satisfied with being a pass or a run next time. ABC, during an Ivy League football game, told us that one team's chance of winning had diminished completely, a clear infraction of the law of diminishing returns (when a team runs back punts and kickoffs for less yardage as the game goes on). In golf, *Sports Illustrated* noted that "a twosome of Bobby Nichols and Lee Trevino talk no more than most pairs—except that Lee does it all." Well, Jim, Howard, Brent, and *Sports Illustrated*, maybe Nichols came to play.

The newspapers are not far behind. The *Pittsburgh Post-Gazette* ran a photograph with the caption "Jimmy Connors gets an unidentified kiss from a local fan." The *Post-Gazette* was trying to say that the woman's name was not given; the kiss, apparently, was standard. A sportswriter for the Lake Charles, Louisiana, *American Press,* covering high-school football, called a team capitalistic. He meant that it turned its opponent's fumbles into touchdowns. Thus the class struggle in Louisiana.

Class attitudes are expressed in a more patrician way in the sports pages of the *Times* of London:

"The weather was a little cooler at Cheltenham yesterday, which helped to make us all better-tempered; and crowds at Cheltenham (the ground nearly full again) need to be good tempered, because handsome though the setting may be, the facilities are on the primitive side. I have not visited the gentlemen's lavatory tent this year, but am assured, by my friends, and indeed by my own nose, that the Ladysmith tradition is preserved. When, in the members' bar, I asked for some water with my whisky, I was told: 'There's a tap round the corner.'

"Still, Cheltenham is Cheltenham, and as one jolly round pink gentleman said to me, pressing a glass of champagne into my hand, under the impression that I was his godson: 'If you want real discomfort here, you have to come to the Gold Cup.' "

And so on. Seven lines later, he begins his account of the cricket match.

I am, I know, mixing up the sports, but I can hardly be blamed. Nowadays a long fly, arching skyward,* will chase an outfielder to the distant wall at the same time that a shifty guard, using a solid pick from a stalwart seven-foot center, drives the middle, a slap shot eludes the masked goalie's desperate lunge as he sprawls on the ice and the red light flashes on behind him, and a tennis player dueling on court does not give the shirt off her back but sells it as advertising space. In these days of short skirts, women players' underpants could carry a plug for, perhaps, radial tires. Women likely to be eliminated in the early round and hence

---

* I am not quite right about the long fly. It arches domeward, because stadiums are increasingly roofed over. With so many Latin-American players in the major leagues, we can imagine the shouted instructions: Look domeward, Angel!

not good investments might be required to carry public service messages: Vote!

Most Americans get their sports news on television, and the broadcasters like to make things crystal clear. So we are told about the team with the worst record in baseball won-and-lostwise, about the football player who incurs a penalty and is the guilty culprit, and about the players who have good success in spite of being plagued by physical injuries. Ralph Kiner has explained why a team may not use a squeeze play to get the man on third base home. The squeeze, he said, might not succeed successfully. The players have the same uneasy feeling that success may be failure. Dave Kingman, outfielder for the New York Mets, expressing his gratification after hitting two home runs off Andy Messersmith, post-studiology and with Atlanta: "I have had terrible success against him in the past."

Just as good success is desired, so are good power and good speed. Maury Wills has described a player as having good running speed. "I knew it was hit good," said Mike Schmidt of the Philadelphia Phillies, "but the ball doesn't carry good in the Astrodome." It carries bad. When James J. Braddock died, there were stories about the fight in which he lost his heavyweight championship to Joe Louis. In the first round Braddock knocked Louis down. Louis got up. Braddock: "I thought if I hit him good, he'll stay down." It did not work out that way. Braddock was a brave man, a light-heavyweight, really, who returned to fighting when he was unemployed and on relief and went on to win the heavyweight championship. He was a longshoreman and uneducated. Tom Seaver of the New York Mets is a college graduate: "Cedeno hit the ball pretty good." Budd Schulberg is a novelist. Said he, after the Ali-Foreman fight, "The fight turned out pretty good."

Good has long been indispensable to sports language:

1. "I guess he means good" (Manager Joe Frazier of the New York Mets about an umpire);

2. "Apparently somebody's controlling the Commissioner pretty good" (Manager Billy Martin of the New York Yankees on Baseball Commissioner Bowie Kuhn);

3. "He ran the curve good" (O. J. Simpson of ABC Sports on Dwayne Evans in the men's 200-metres at the Montreal Olympics); and

4. "Evelyn Ashford comes from behind very good" (Wyomia Tyus on the women's 100-metre dash at Montreal)

I believe that a change is in the making, but good has a few seasons left.

"I think we'll have a pretty good year," says the coach who knows that doom awaits but doesn't want to damage morale in the interim.

"We'll have a good season," says the coach who thinks his team may go all the way but prefers not to say so.

Now, the coach who is full of confidence or, in the words of Tom Landry, coach of the Dallas Cowboys, whose confidence factor is up: "All the players have real good attitudes, we have some real good prospects, including one boy who is going to be a real good kicker, and I think we'll have a real good season."

During the 1976 baseball season Reggie Jackson, after his first game for the Baltimore Orioles, reported that it felt good, because he was moving good and taking the pitches good. The pitches Jackson took did not come from Mickey Lolich, because Detroit had traded him to the New York Mets of the National League. After his second victory for the Mets, Lolich acknowledged that he was old for a pitcher—thirty-five—but, he said, "I still throw pretty good." When Gus Ganakas, basketball coach at Michigan State University, suspended ten players, he did not give up hope of getting them back on the squad. "I feel good compassion between us," he said. Bad compassion, Ganakas must have sensed, had been the downfall of many basketball coaches.

Since sports language has moved into politics, good has followed. Governor Hugh Carey of New York has spoken of a particular development as a good probability. Other kinds are the poor probability and the probability that is out of the question. During the 1976 primary campaign the *New York Times* reported that when Senator Henry Jackson mentioned Daniel P. Moynihan as a possible Secretary of State, he usually drew good applause.

Good applause is well meant and honorably intended. Bad applause should be rejected out of, so to speak, hand.

Politicians aren't the only good guys. Advertisers are also. We have it from Bill Cosby that "Ford-built means a lot of things that are good-built." In a television commercial for Manischewitz wine, Sammy Davis, Jr., announced, "I'm into wines pretty good," and Coca-Cola has a drink called Mr. PiBB, with the advertising slogan "It goes down good." Faced with an objection to the slogan, a Coca-Cola executive replied that the company was aiming at a target audience and liked to think it could relate to the "young even at the cost of using a phrase that is a 'put-on.' " The executive did not say who pays the cost. Coca-Cola doesn't.

Politicians and advertisers may discover that they are on the scene too late. A new generation of broadcasters has already moved beyond good to better things. Consider the former quarterback John Unitas. Unitas has three things to say about a player: He did a fine job. He did a real fine job. He did a super job. About entire teams, or categories of players such as offensive guards, he also has three things to say: They do a fine job. They do a real fine job. They do a super job. No mention of good.

Good shots are disappearing from golf. If a player hits a nine-iron shot to the green, the broadcaster will say, "That was a real fine shot." Sometimes, because he believes the audience is confused about the ball and the green and thinks the game on the screen is water polo, he will say, "That was a real fine golf shot." In exceptional cases, "That was a super shot."

Super is branching out—Colonel Arvid E. West, Jr., commander of cadet basic training at West Point, said of the first women cadets, "They're doing super—but it won't last." Not with real super waiting to be waved in. Moreover, winner of the 1976 Masters tournament Raymond Floyd has blazed a new trail. Before the final round Floyd was asked how he had slept. "I slept terrific," he said. There is always something grander beyond the horizon. In 1974, when the World Series was under way, in progress, and continuing in California, Vin Scully said on NBC about Reggie Jackson: "Granted he has a strong arm velocitywise, it's not so accurate." This entire nation knows what is meant when an outfielder is said to have a strong arm, but velocitywise adds a new dimension to our studiology. The California pitcher Nolan Ryan noted one day during 1976 spring training that he had good velocity. He understated it. Ryan has real good velocity. He is very fast.

I sometimes wonder—this may be regarded as a digression— whether there is not another accomplishment players must have if they are to last in the major leagues. This is the ability to spit with good velocity when the television camera is on them. It seems clear that a method of communication has been worked out between the television crews and the players. This is not necessary when a player is close enough to see the red light that means the camera is transmitting a picture on the air, but when he isn't, I suppose his instructions come from somebody in the television crew, perhaps by Navy semaphore flags. As soon as he gets the message, he shifts his tobacco or chewing gum and lets go.

Another possibility is that there is no arrangement* between the television crews and the players but that the players themselves have designated somebody in the dugout who is not otherwise occupied to watch the cameras and to wigwag to any players who may be in the camera's view. Perhaps this assignment is given to injured players as a way of keeping them involved in the club's fortunes. Whatever the method employed, it rarely fails. Camera on player or coach or manager, and out comes the oyster. Why does it? Spitting is thought to be a sign of virility, unless it results from a cough or a cold.

Twenty-three spittoo.

All is not lost in sports broadcasting. It is a matter of getting the right people on the job. It is easy to find someone, almost always an ex-player or ex-coach, who will say, "They're a very physical team"† and "I think they're up for this one," or a whimsi-

---

* Or prearrangement, which comes even earlier, as preplanning comes before planning and prerecorded programs are recorded before recorded programs are.

† This is why there are physical injuries.

cal one who will refer to the end zone in football as royal soil,* the linebackers as the containment committee, and the referee as the chief of the spheroid shylocks. Those who tell you that teams deck other teams, or slam, squeeze past, down, clip, rout, outlast, skin, rock, or thump them, while notching another win or upping their mark to whatever the mark is upped to, are thick on the ground.

I learned early about clichés of sports. In the fall of 1941 I was a member of the Washington bureau of International News Service (later to be merged with United Press in United Press International). That puts it grandly. I was a copy boy, a position that would now be called at NBC News a desk assistant. I hope it makes a difference. When passes were available for sports events that INS had no intention of covering, copy boys were able to use them. This meant that you could sit in the press box and pretend to be a reporter, and then call in a brief account of the game in case the desk man in charge wanted to use it.

That fall I was given the credentials for the football game between George Washington and, as I recall, Georgetown. It was a game of no interest between teams of no distinction whatever, and it ended in a scoreless tie.

I telephoned.

"What was the score?" the desk man asked.

"There was no score."

"Struggled to a scoreless tie, did they?" the desk man said.

I looked at my notes. Struggled to a scoreless tie was what I had written. The desk man saved me the embarrassment of admitting it or the trouble of finding a substitute. "I don't think we need it," he said.

My experiences were not always that unhappy. Once I was given a ringside seat for a heavyweight fight. A new man in the

---

* Royal soil used to be pay dirt, and backs would tote the pigskins into pay dirt, leaving would-be tacklers in their wake like so much flotsam and jetsam, who used to play opposite defensive ends for the Naperville, Illinois, Rapiers.

bureau, who outranked me, which was not hard to do, asked for the seat. I was moved back twenty or thirty rows. During the fight one of the boxers broke the other's nose. Blood spattered onto the suit of the man who had taken my seat. Those were days when I thought not merely twice but repeatedly about the cost of having a suit cleaned. Justice, it seemed to me, had triumphed. Copy boys were not to be pushed around.

Sports reporting is full of manufactured good cheer and catch phrases. I prefer natural eloquence, even when it goes wrong. Mendy Rudolph, who used to be a referee in the National Basketball Association, has become a color man* and analyst of NBA games for CBS. Rudolph has assessed two teams as very equal, and on another occasion, during a game between the Phoenix Suns and the Kansas City Kings, he stunned the play-by-play announcer, Don Criqui, by asking him, "That basket—how round is it?"

Criqui: How round is it?

Rudolph: Yes. How round is it?

After a while Criqui deduced that Rudolph was asking him the size of the basket, what its diameter was. It turned out to be eighteen inches. The Rudolph-Criqui exchange was the most interesting part of the game.

The words, "Let's reminisce about tomorrow night's fight," were uttered by a former fight manager, Vic Marsillo, who had a radio show in Newark, New Jersey. They tell us what sports broadcasting could be, and such colorful language should not be confused with poor grammar—"Our listeners may wonder why they can't run the ball easilier" and "He pursuited him very good on that play." Or with pomposity—"He is bigger, from the standpoint of physical proportions," and "The Jets maintain their hands on the football." Boxing managers, a strange and wonderful tribe, may be the great hope.

Here I must apologize for a mistake in my first book on

---

* Color men and color women supply quips, statistics, historical references, and, it is fondly believed, a dash of personality.

language, *Strictly Speaking*. I attributed the remark "I was in a transom" to Joe Jacobs, who was the American manager of the German heavyweight Max Schmeling. I thought that Jacobs had said it after Schmeling lost a decision to Jack Sharkey at Yankee Stadium in 1932. Harry Markson, who promoted fights in Madison Square Garden for many years, wrote to tell me that Jacobs was not the author of that mighty line. According to Markson, it was the heavyweight King Levinsky, who accounted for his poor showing against Joe Louis with the explanation that he had been in a transom. There were stories at the time that so intimidating were Louis's person and reputation, and so deep in consequence Levinsky's transom, that his manager, his sister Lena Levinsky, known with sports-page inevitability as Leaping Lena, had to force Levinsky into the ring at the point of a gun. The fight lasted two minutes, twenty-one seconds.

Markson sent along some lines, spoken by managers of his acquaintance, that in natural eloquence rank with Levinsky's. Managers usually refer to their fighters as boys, and one, on hearing that another manager's fighter had run out on him, thought he should say something kind about his own, who had stayed with him in good times and bad. "My boy," he said, "has always been fatal to me." Another came in one day to tell Markson that his boy was suffering from a crink in his back and a throbble in his side.

"Will he be able to fight tonight?" Markson asked.

Said the manager, "It's problemental."

Having apologized, I think I should explain how I came to attribute to Joe Jacobs a remark made by King Levinsky. I can explain by summarizing a news story:

A prisoner on trial on charges of attempted murder and armed robbery walked out of the Queens House of Detention for Men yesterday morning in place of another inmate who had completed a fifteen-day sentence for petit larceny but was, he said, asleep at release time. It was the second such erroneous release in the past ten months at the jail.

Correction Commissioner Benjamin J. Malcolm ordered an

investigation by his department's inspector general. "It would appear to me," Malcolm said, "that there was slippage."

That's how I came to make the mistake. Slippage.

More riches than are suspected lie in the language of sportswriters, if only they could be mined. I have been told of a game that sportswriters play to pass the time and that could enliven baseball broadcasts. It consists of asking a question not concerned with baseball and answering it with a line usually delivered by baseball announcers:

"How is your husband feeling, Countess?"

"The Count remains the same."

"Why are the flags being raised for the President's inauguration?"

"It's an obvious bunting situation."

"What will we do with this messy pile of Greek books?"

"Homer here will tie it up."

It's catching. I tried a couple.

"What happened to the handle on this jug?"

"He really broke that one off."

"I could swear we had another bottle of wine."

"That one is gone."

We have seen how sports language, as in good speed, spreads to politics, as in good applause. A basketball coach worries about being outsized and outquicked. Jimmy Carter's national campaign manager, Hamilton Jordan, had the same concern. "In every area," Jordan said during the 1976 primary campaign, "candidate's time, money, and staff depth, we are in danger of being out-resourced." If that was so, Carter must have had inner resources. I once spoke to an organization of young businessmen with an extensive educational program. In one of the courses the organization advised its members, "Nationally-known resources are available throughout the week for face-to-face discussions." At the Republican convention in Miami Beach in 1972, I had dinner in a restaurant where another of the diners was Rogers Morton, then Secretary of the Interior. Morton came over to say hello and was introduced to the others at the table. One of them was the young daughter of an NBC producer. When Morton left she said in delight, "I met a Secretary!" What might she have said if she had met a Resource? For that same 1972 convention E. Howard Hunt, one of the Watergate burglars, had plans for kidnaping unfriendly demonstrators. The "human resources side" of his work, he called it. The demonstrators would have been out-resourced and out of town.

The mingling of language in sports and public affairs may also be seen in the well-known political epithet, left-leaning. Sometimes, when a pitcher picks a runner off first base, he will explain, "I caught him leaning." This means that the runner, possibly the well-known base stealer Art Theft, defying the rifle-armed catcher Art Sleuth, was leaning toward second base, hoping to get a real good jump and steal second. The pitcher whirls and throws to first, and the runner, leaning the wrong way, that is, right, and delayed in returning to first base, is tagged out.

There are occasions, however, when it works the other way. If you are leading off a base but leaning left when the ball is hit, you are going to be slower getting to the next base. This may, in sports language, cost you. In political language it should have been costed out beforehand. In baseball, as in politics, there are times to lean left and times to lean right and times to lean not at all.

Pitchers lean, also. A left-handed pitcher, or southpaw, may lean left, or south, against a left-handed batter and deliver the ball from as far to the side as he can. This leads the batter to pull away from the plate—put his foot in the bucket is the term that swims back from youth—whereupon the curve, which is what the canny left-hander has delivered, sweeps over for a strike. A canny right-handed pitcher may use the tactic on a right-handed batter. For either pitcher the effect is compounded if he throws side-arm, which makes the lean more pronounced. The ball he delivers then goes under the terrifying name of cross fire.

For the batter, there is an advantage in being a switch hitter, one who faces a left-handed pitcher batting right-handed and a right-handed pitcher batting left-handed. The pitchers then, lean they ever so determinedly, will find that it avails them naught.

Many pitchers found themselves in this position when facing the distinguished switch hitter of the New York Yankees, Mickey Mantle. "What did it avail you?" they would be asked as they trudged off the mound, and the reply they gave was, "Naught."

Nowadays the conversation is much the same after they face Pete Rose of the Cincinnati Reds, who not only switches but crouches fiercely. "Say not the struggle naught availeth," pitchers are implored after facing Rose. You know the reply. However, there are few switch hitters. For most batters the task remains the same. It is to dig in their heels, stand up like men, and turn back the challenge from both extremes. There is a lesson here for all of us.

In the dear, dead days not quite beyond recall, the Brooklyn Dodgers had an ambidextrous pitcher named Pea Ridge Day. Day was something like Ring Lardner's celebrated infielder who couldn't hit but couldn't field either. Leaning left or right, he had trouble getting them out with either arm.

Washington language does in sports what it does in Washington—makes things sound more complicated. After the New York Knicks of the National Basketball Association lost one night to the Detroit Pistons, New York's coach, Red Holzman, complained about the officials. "They lived up to their capabilities," Holzman said. "They did exactly what I thought they would." Said Moe Finkelstein, football coach at Thomas Jefferson High School, in New York City, after his team went through a season undefeated, "This year, we won every game in a different way and had to use all our capabilities."

Capability came, as far as I can trace it, from the world of business,* where companies with even the faintest hope of being viable and major recognized the need for overall capabilities, systems capabilities, generating capabilities, in-house capabilities, phase-in capabilities, and, in a changing world, flexibility capa-

---

* I do not mean to imply that capability is a new word. The British architect and landscape gardener Lancelot Brown (1716–1783) used the word so often he has gone down in history as Capability Brown.

bilities. People on public payrolls in Washington phased it in in-house.

President Ford had barely taken office when he sat down with television reporters, one of whom asked him whether he had the brains to be President. On the man-bites-dog principle, Ford would have had to say that he didn't. No other answer would have produced news. Ford chose the harder way. "My feeling of security, my feeling of certainty grows every day," he said. "I feel very secure in the capability that I have to do the job." He could have said, "Yes, I can do it," or even "Yes," but either was too meager for Washington. When it came out that the CIA had been told to pass $6,000,000 to certain Italian political parties, Ron Nessen announced that Ford was angry because he thought that such disclosures "undermine our capability to carry out our foreign policy."

I have asked myself to the extent of my capability to put questions that I am willing to answer, why ability does not serve. It is for the same reason that serve no longer serves and is being replaced by service, as in the case of an organization that offers to service you with facts, statistics, and graphics. President Ford told a group of mayors early in 1976 that his administration wanted to give them the ability and the capability to deal with their problems. The mayors, who had been prepared to settle for either, must have been overwhelmed.

Nobody is more devoted to capability than the CIA. It had, according to the Senate Intelligence Committee report on assassination plots, a stand-by assassination capability (useful for knocking off old stand-bys who outlive their usefulness) which involved incapacitating, eliminating, terminating, removing from the scene, and altering the health of those on whom the capability was to be demonstrated.

The stand-by part is important. It will be remembered that in the opera *Rigoletto,* when Rigoletto wants the Duke of Mantua killed because the Duke has seduced Rigoletto's daughter, Gilda, he has no stand-by assassination capability of his own and turns, therefore, to Sparrafucile, an assassin for hire. However, Sparrafucile, at the urging of his sister, Maddalena, who has been charmed by the Duke, agrees not to kill the Duke, provided somebody else assassinable turns up at his country inn, and to pass off that body as the Duke's. This proves to be Gilda, who sacrifices herself so that the Duke may live. It will be seen that Verdi and his librettist, Piave, even in 1851—and before them Victor Hugo, who in 1832 wrote the play *Le Roi S'amuse,* on which the opera was based—were arguing that a stand-by assassination capability was essential if the work was to be well and carefully done.

Stand-by assassination capability is an element of covert capability, which conflicts with yet another capability, that of oversight. If the CIA has covert capability and Congress has oversight capability, which will be the more capable? This will depend on whether Congress's oversight capability includes veto capability. If it doesn't, Congress's oversight capability will merely lull it into a sense of false security, a sense on whose behalf, if we are to believe the columnists and editorial writers, lulling is incessant.

It will come as no surprise to anyone familiar with Washington that capability was quickly deemed to be insufficient. In his State of the Union message of January 1976, President Ford asked for an intelligence capability that would be effective, as though effectiveness were not what capability implied, and he asked that it be responsible and responsive as well. Ernest Gellhorn, dean of the College of Law at Arizona State University, and senior counsel to the Rockefeller Commission on CIA activities, wanted the oversight capability to be permanent and well staffed. Statements of this kind alarmed the columnist William Safire, who demanded that we "put the spotlight of pitiless publicity on oversight's lush patronage." Otherwise, he said, "We are condoning the concealment of a dagger of venality beneath a cloak of reform." This was precisely what Sparrafucile did and explains the false sense of security into which Rigoletto was lulled.

If the federal system is to thrive, capability cannot be confined to Washington. The Illinois Board of Education, for example, anticipates having model-creating and coalescence capability:

"The purpose of this project is to develop the capability for institutions of higher learning and community agencies and organizations to coalesce for the development of community services and create a model for services that would maximize the available resources from a number of institutions and provide communication and priority needs and responses to the educational needs of a given community."

In the world of the social sciences, the compulsion to create a model is all but universal.

"We're creating a model."

*"We're* creating a model."

"Our model is coalescing, and maximizing."

"Our model provides communication and priority needs and responses. It has the capability."

Capability exists beyond given communities and even as far afield as Rhodesia, in southern Africa. There the government spokesman, Edward Sutton-Pryce, said that Rhodesia had developed and was producing a combat vehicle with "counterambush and countermine capabilities." This last describes a condition in which the mine goes off under the counter.

I do not mean to leave capability in southern Africa, especially because a new species of it has turned up in Washington, this being unprecedented capability, a quality the Army claims for its new main battle tank, the XM-1. The XM-1's unprecedented capability is to take a hit and survive. Add agility, cross-country mobility, and a new compartmentalization design, and the Army believes that the XM-1 will have great battlefield survivability. If the flag is to continue to fly o'er the rampartmentalization we watch, survival capability at the preoverrun figure of $1,024,000 per tank seems not too much to ask.

President Ford has said that American ballistic missiles are more accurate than the Soviet Union's, and "much more survivable." That sounds as though the missiles could be more readily survived by their intended victims if they were used, but that is not what Ford meant. Survivable retaliatory capability is what he meant. He was using shorthand.

What has the State Department been doing while the Department of Defense develops tanks of unprecedented capability? The State Department has been tailoring a centralized focus for consumer interests and fashioning a viable blueprint for consumer participation,* with a capability that rests on inputs, outputs, and thruputs. An input is simple enough: It goes in. An output comes out. And a thruput? Just tell it, please, State Department, in your own words:

"Information inputs from consumers, thruputs between initiating parties and potential users, and outputs from the Department properly occur in varying degrees and at varying levels in this process. Inputs are directed toward existing or prospective programs, and can be solicited or unsolicited. Thruputs—a critical element in the Department's mode of operation—are manifested by interaction between the international community and the U.S. public and private sectors. Outputs are designed to educate and/or reply to the consuming public."

Thruputs may be critical elements in everybody's mode of operation, but most of us don't realize that we are launching them. Here is a perfectly balanced interactive thruput:

"Good morning, John. How are you?"

"Well, thank you. And you?"

A thruput of the kind the State Department has in mind is more complex:

"Hello, operator. This is the U.S. private sector. The international community, please. International community? U.S. private sector here. Let us go forward together in hard but friendly competition, with the peoples of the world reaping the benefit in lower prices and higher standards of living, secure in the knowledge that the quest for peace through mutual understanding goes on." Since interaction is required, the international community

---

* In 1972 there was something that sounded like this in the Nixon Administration. It was called Operation Responsiveness, and it tailored a centralized focus and fashioned a viable blueprint to enable federal agencies to help in Nixon's reelection campaign.

responds by speaking of removing artificial barriers to trade and of stimulating the free exchange of ideas, thus realizing the higher aspirations common to all mankind. The thruput is complete. In sports terms, they were shadowboxing. Neither laid a glove on the other.

Anything more in the State Department's own words? Yes, the Department had a few linkages left over from the nuclear arms negotiations with the Soviet Union. Wherefore:

"The introduction of the 'consumer communications channel,' as monitored by the Consumer Affairs Coordinator, will provide the linkage to enhance the effectiveness of these ongoing efforts."* The announcement also spoke of utilization of professional public opinion analysts to input consumer attitudes throughout the Department.† It concluded: "A special effort is being made by the Department to assure that Federal Register Items are clear, as brief as possible, free from jargon, and timely."‡ For this relief from jargon, much thanks.

I have not asked Representative Brock Adams of Washington whether he would stand with the State Department on input/output/thruput, but my guess is that he would. At the beginning of 1975, Adams became chairman of the House budget committee. At the beginning of 1976 he told a reporter, "My input quantum jumped tremendously in the past year in the ability to get things

---

* Linkage is what the second baseman provides in the continuum of a short to second to first double play. Ongoing efforts are needed in any sport, but especially in baseball. It's a long season.

† Forty-four per cent of the fans in the park thought the manager acted wisely in using a pinch hitter, 33 per cent thought he was foolish to do it so early in the game, and the remaining 23 per cent either had no opinion or were listening to a broadcast of the game on transistor radios and did not want to be disturbed. One fan who was shouting, "Get that bum outa there," was recorded as abstaining.

‡ We all know about the player who does not get many hits, though the ones he gets are timely, coming when his team is at bat. They are free from jargon, not being called bingles or safeties, and also as brief as possible, usually getting the timely one only as far as first base, where he remains while the next three men go down in order.

done."* Having an input quantum to be reckoned with is the successor to that wistful favorite of yesteryear, making a meaningful contribution,† and for a politician it can be a call to arms: "My opponent tells you that he can do more for this state than I can, but my input quantum was impacting the national decision-making process when the people of this state needed it. Where was his?"‡

I have assumed that an input quantum impacts the decision-making process rather than being inserted in it. This may be quite wrong. Inserting inputs seems more logical and, although this has the dysteleological effect of keeping the inputs from ever becoming outputs, so does outserting them. Outserting is already taking place at the Ford Foundation, in New York, where an executive told me that in the same mail delivery that brought him notice of a meeting of college and university administrators devoted to creative retrenchment§ he received a requisition which, in the course of a job description, employed outsert, as in, he assumed, "First outsert the plug from the wall." When enough people outsert themselves, we may be in the presence of an outpour, this being what the Secretary of Housing and Urban Development, Carla Hills, believed might come about if the trickle of suburban families back to the cities could be encouraged. Encouraged Mrs. Hills believed it should be, so that the cities would "attract a heterogeneous people mix and . . . broaden their opportunities for leveraging funds." Are you a heterogeneous person? With leverageable funds? Welcome to our mix.

Outserting a plug from the wall leads, naturally, to an outage. Outages defy climatic differences. The Associated Press reported

---

* Input quantum sets me humming Stephen Foster's "Camptown Races":
    "De input quantum sing dis song, Doo dah! Doo dah!
     De input quantum's five mile long, Oh! Doo dah day!"
  † I know I can help this club.
  ‡ When did he ever get the most valuable player award?
  § First we have to contain their offense. Then we can think about scoring some points of our own.

one in Bethel, Alaska, where fire destroyed the municipal power plant, and United Press International reported more than one in Panama City Beach, Florida, after Hurricane Eloise passed through. UPI also reported an outage that hit Sacramento, causing the state legislature to stop work and many state employees to be sent home, which was a shame because the Sacramento Municipal Utility District had, until then, an excellent inage image. On December 24, 1974, the University of Pittsburgh, known to itself as the Cathedral of Learning, posted a sign announcing an elevator outage. This suggests that the principal justification for the university's regarding itself as a cathedral of learning is that it is in a high-rise building. High-rise buildings, by the way, used to be tall.*

I have no evidence that the University of Pittsburgh has gone this far, but there are places where two or more signs, taken together, are known as signage. The Sisters of Providence, of Holyoke, Massachusetts, announced in a newsletter completion of a study of the signage needs of the area. That was in October 1974, and the Sisters may have established a precedent. A year later, after moving to its new world headquarters in East Hanover, New Jersey, the National Biscuit Company advised its employees that increased signage was needed in the building and that signage would also be added above the cafeteria counters. Countersign capability.

Signage and outage I expect to arrive in baseball shortly, probably shepherded by Howard Cosell, who said during a football game that the New York Giants faced the problem of the stoppage of O. J. Simpson. (The blockage by the Buffalo linemen made the problem more difficult.) The catcher will be flashing signage to the pitcher, and the third-base coach to the runners, and the umpires will be giving the ball and strike and fair ball and foul signage, and declaring "Outage at first" unless the runner is viable. When players misbehave, they will be output of the game. A manager will send signage to the bullpen for a relief pitcher to

---

* It's a high-rise fly, about fifteen stories up, just inside the left-field line. The left fielder is under it, and he has it.

input after outserting the starter, against whom the opposition has been registering thruputs almost at will, five in the first inning alone, which is a large quantum to overcome. In the first inning there were five thruputs, six successful impactions of bat on ball, and two slippages. Two potential thruputs were left on.

It is my observation that in Washington, and elsewhere, there are far more inputs than there are outputs. This means that a large number of puts are disappearing somewhere in the process. God knows where they'll eventually turn up. It came to pass in the city of the input quantum that a job was available at the Federal Communications Commission, where employees who were interested were invited to submit their applications on Form A-136, "Application for Position Vacancy," rather as rookies and free agents are invited to a team's training camp. Applying for a vacancy rather than the position itself seems pointless, but it is of no moment: any government agency would rather say position vacancy than vacant position. The job was that of Word Processing Supervisor in the Word Processing Center of the Office of the Bureau Chief of the Broadcast Bureau, a noncritical sensitive position requiring security clearance, in which incumbent has total management responsibility for the operations of the Word Processing Center, so as to achieve maximum utilization of personnel and equipment, and timely, accurate, and cost-effective accomplishment of Word Processing Center objectives within the constraints established.

I am an experienced reporter, but I did no digging and thus no investigative work to learn what word processing centers are. I thought they might be printing plants or offices where all government statements are emulsified.* Not so. My knowledge of them I owe to a government employee in Washington who sent me a

---

* A story was told just after the Second World War about American and British correspondents waiting for the Italian government to issue its *épuration* law, the law under which collaborators with the Nazis would be dealt with. There was a delay, and some of the correspondents wondered aloud what the purifiers were doing. An American reporter, Homer Bigart, had an explanation. "Putting in the loopholes," he said.

copy of the FCC vacancy announcement. On request, he then sent me job descriptions. My next letter had a plaintive tone. "Is there anything available," I asked, "that explains what word processing is?"

"A word processing unit," my benefactor wrote back, "is a typing pool. Happy New Year."

Less pretentiously, the typing pool used to be called the bullpen. In baseball, the bullpen coach speaks on the telephone to the manager in the dugout, telling him which of his relief pitchers has good stuff, which one looks ready, and how long he thinks any of them can go. A comparable junior executive in the Word Processing Center could tell the Word Processing Supervisor whether Ms. Bright was at the top of her form and could deal with a tricky memorandum, or whether he should call on Mr. Hapgood, slower at the keyboard ("He doesn't have good speed") but steady and experienced and not likely to be rattled. Hapgood probably could use another day's rest, since he has lately been processing out of rotation because Mrs. Ewen came down with a sore arm and had to miss a couple of turns, but Hapgood's stamina is legendary and he is a sure bet for the Word Processing Hall of Fame.

Among the Word Processing Supervisor's subordinate incumbents, there is one who has the duty of correcting inadvertent errors in grammar, I suppose while letting the deliberate ones go. Others process a large volume of documents, including correspondence, memorandums, reports, agenda items, etc. Still others are known as specialists in document creation. I had long wondered where the documents came from for archives, for presidential libraries, for leaking, for losing and pilfering, for tugs-of-war between executive departments and congressional committees, for publication in the *New York Times;* for photostating and microfilming; for classifying and, once in a great while, declassifying; for filling large buildings, smaller temporary structures, and briefcases; for circulating within and across departmental lines; for keeping from scholars until a stated time has passed. The existence of the document creators solves the mystery. Richard Nixon was able to claim ownership of 42,000,000 documents when he left the White House. It was not an abnormal number. Since then, twenty-five tons of papers, packed in 1660 boxes, from the Reagan Administration in California have been given to Stanford University, which shows what can be done with fewer resources at the state level.

Government employees are not thought to be among the nation's most industrious workers. This surely maligns the document creators. It also maligns those word processors who wait, pad and pencil at the ready, for the heady order: "Take a document."

# Some Enchanted
# Citadel

A concept was delivered to me one day, by mail, with nothing on the envelope to indicate what lay within. The top page of the enclosure bore these words:

WESTERN INSTITUTE OF AVIATION
A Concept

and I closed the door and lowered the blinds before reading further. I reproduce here only the Introductory Statement:

"Aviation services and their impact now have great dimensions. With appreciation of the facts—including that only great things can have great faults and that perfection takes some time—oversimplification can be misleading. Improved communications are vital if aviation is to attain the full measure of its possible greatness.

"We trust, that by joining together the many specialist groups who make the system work—who have treated technical problems as opportunities—and who have achieved, for a majority of people, a quality of service that tends to satiate the recipients to a point approaching apathy, we may treat the opposition so as not to inflame the anti-aviation enthusiasts, but to convert them.

"Toward finding better ways to work out our problems, we offer the Western Institute of Aviation for broadening the base of understanding, evolving a means of lifting up our eyes and objectives and, hopefully, realizing our mutual interdependence in optimizing aviation services to people through the synergism of our efforts."

That concept was passed on to me by the director of airport planning in a large western city, whose help was being solicited but who had been satiated to a point beyond apathy.

Another concept reached me on an otherwise ordinary day in a letter from an instructional television center in a large city in Texas. It was the concept of human possibilities, which is a concept to reckon with. I was flattered to be told about this concept because the writer of the letter said that he was looking for extraordinary people in various fields who were using their potential to the fullest and who were willing to be interviewed on film for an instructional television course in the humanities.

Egomania drove me on:

"Here is the question we would like to ask you in a brief interview:

"Can you isolate a single moment in your life as *the* most fulfilling?

"Or put another way:

"What moment(s) did you feel most successful as a person?

"If you are familiar with the psychologist Abraham Maslow, you will know we are talking about 'self-actualizing' people, people who are being fully human.

"We hope the question intrigues you. Your answers can greatly help our students explore their own self-expectations."

Glowing, I reread the letter, only to find that I was not sufficiently extraordinary for the purpose, since, although I self-actualize madly, I do not use my potential to the fullest but only to the full. Reluctantly, I declined.

In public relations and in advertising, a concept is an idea that has become important. An expert in the field can spot the precise moment when the transformation takes place. It was, for example, the moment when the golf glove incorporated Iso-massage action to relieve tiredness in the hand, the better to grip Strata-bloc woods with cycolac inserts, and irons built with true-temper step-down steel shafts. Calling ideas concepts is itself a concept, and the greatestest thing of its kind since a conversation became a dialogue.

The potency of concepts is now widely recognized. A New York furniture store changed its name to Interconcepts. A public relations company put this advertisement in the *Wall Street Journal*: "Somewhere is someone who knows that our business is not a matter of placements, releases and contact. Someone who knows that professional PR, like professional advertising and promotion, is really a matter of strong, creative marketing communications concepts. Concepts that establish a singular identity for a company, a product or a service. Concepts that impact upon marketplaces, and hopefully industries as well." Marketplaces may profit from being impacted on by concepts, but hopefully industries have nothing in stock but good will, which they pick up for a song, usually Jerome Kern's "Look for the Silver Lining," from companies going bankrupt. They spend much of their time in wishful thinking, and the fact is that concepts are wasted on them. They need the attitude expressed in the song written by Jay Gorney and Ralph Harrison, Junior, for the thirtieth anniversary of the publication *PR News*:

What's the most exciting profession in our land?
It's PR, PR, PR.
What is most important for our people to understand?
It's PR, PR, PR.
What needs education
In our wonderful nation?

> What, in our country, is destined to expand?
> It's Public Relations!
>
> CHORUS:
> Yes, we are
> Mighty PRoud to be in our PR.
> Yes, we are
> All doing our job well up to par
> We live and love our thriving profession
> One which can help overcome recession
> Yes, we are
> All PRoud to be in our PR. . . .

That shows how a song can arouse enthusiasm. This was part of the plan when President Ford launched the Whip Inflation Now, or WIN, campaign shortly after he took office. Dedicated enemies of inflation were to show it no mercy by wearing lapel buttons that said WIN, and the coup de grâce was to be administered by a song by Meredith Willson, composer of *The Music Man*. The song said that the nation did not need inflation and that you were going to pass it by and so was I.

The campaign foundered early, probably because the buttons lacked the killer instinct, and so Meredith Willson's song never had the opportunity to turn the tide. There was a faint echo of WIN across the Atlantic, where the British, aping the American craze for acronyms, came up with NORM, the National Optimism Revival Movement. When appearing in public, NORM's members proposed to smile, thus helping Britain out of its economic difficulties. NORM had no more effect than WIN did, but it was run by a resident of Leighton Buzzard, Bedfordshire, from a shed in his garden, and cost less.

I have never heard of a song about advertising, but otherwise the difference between advertising and public relations, so far as language goes, is nonmajor. Both set out to do the same thing—create desires and expectations, make people want something, leading them to believe that the world is more exciting than it is. Advertising language is more extravagant, but public relations and advertising are so close that they could be billed with nothing more than 'n' between them, like listings for macaroni 'n' cheese, chips 'n' dips, soup 'n' sandwiches; for neighborhood taverns called Surf 'n' Turf, Beef 'n' Bottle, Booze 'n' Board; for combination service stations and cafés called Tank 'n' Tummy; for houses or boats that bear the owners' names, like Dot 'n' Dave; for real estate developments called Hill 'n' Dale; 'n' Bell 'n' Howell's— pardon, Bell & Howell's—trade-in offer known as Switch 'n' Swap.

You may not think it to look at it, but 'n' is a concept. Actually, 'n is a concept. One letter and one apostrophe, taken together, suggest friendliness, informality, and no high prices. The second ' is always left out. I put in the second ' only to be 'n'noying.

There was a time when someone who wanted a home looked at apartments and houses. Now the choice is among concepts. I had a choice between, on the one hand, one of America's most exciting living concepts (a bold concept and landmark for our times, where the facilities created a total concept of leisure and an ambiance that would become synonymous with my way of life and an integral part of my exciting lifestyle) and, on the other, the world's most splendidly complete lifestyle in an enchanted citadel (a luxurious retreat with a unique vantage point, where life takes on a new richness and serenity, and where life is a banquet and you are the guest of honor because of a concept of service that frees rare and discerning people from the mundane task of providing for their own security and comfort).

Had I been willing to move to a suburb, I could have bought a condoflex with the fabulous Westchester lifestyle. Texas tried to attract me by designating the Dallas/Fort Worth area a metropolitan complex and calling it the Metroplex. In Florida I could have had lifestyle living, which I have not seen offered anywhere else. However, I stayed in New York and chose the landmark for our times because it had one more concept than its rival, the citadel (which thereupon became disenchanted), and because I was looking for a two-concept apartment at the time. With one concept facing south.

Concepts abound in Washington and, as befits the welfare state we are becoming, are often comforting. In December 1975 the head of the United States Consumer Product Safety Commission, Richard O. Simpson, wrote to President Ford that he did not want to be considered for reappointment. Simpson's term had run out in October, and he had not been able to learn what the White House intended to do with him. "I have been singularly unsuccessful in these attempts at communication," he told Ford, though he would hardly have been in a position to know whether his lack of success was singular. "I can only conclude, therefore, that for reasons as yet undisclosed my candidacy is not viable and that there is no specific timetable for resolution." The nonviable candidacy with no specific timetable for resolution is far preferable to being fired. It is a concept.

The CIA has in its arsenal a dart gun with silencer attached which it calls a nondiscernible microbionoculator. It is a concept that reflects the CIA's generosity to its potential victims. We all have our pride, and almost anyone the CIA felt it necessary to render nonviable would prefer being dispatched with a nondiscernible microbionoculator to being shot with a dart gun. Concepts lend dignity while obscuring intent.

ABC television now and then repeats programs, calling them special encore performances, though the calls of "Encore!" are supplied by the network like the laughs on a laugh track. Physicians, when treating mental patients who are not separated from other mental patients, may say that they are receiving milieu therapy. It sounds like something W. C. Fields might have invented:

"Do you practice milieu therapy everywhere, Doctor?"

"No. Only within these purlieus."

"How do your patients react to it?"

"They tell me they feel like a milieu."

To produce a concept, someone, somewhere, must conceptualize, a considerable, even electrifying advance on having conceived. There is a scientific term for two persons conceptualizing the same concept simultaneously. It is synchronicity. Such a phenomenon brought forth the twin concepts of acoustical perfume 'n sonorous design. Acoustical perfume is a background noise intended to sound like the noise produced by a ventilating system. It is used in large office spaces as a substitute for partitions, and is played just loudly enough to permit private conversations. The noise that does come out of a ventilating system is not suitable for the purpose because it is not a concept. Also, the president of the company that sells acoustical perfume says that noise is too negative a word for the environmentally oriented. Handsome does as handsome is.

Sonorous design is produced by Muzak, the background (and sometimes the foreground) music company, which recently passed its forty-second birthday, to my intense regret. Muzak calls its employees "specialists in the physiological and psychological applications of music" and estimates that they apply it to 60,000,000 people a day. I speak as one who does not want to have music applied to him, physiologically or psychologically, but those of my persuasion are being borne under. The chairman of the board of scientific advisers of Muzak, a Ph.D. in industrial psychology, has said: "Among the interrelated matters of a time and place, Muzak is a thing that fits in. The things that go together, including the Muzak, are synomorphs." Synomorphs, so far as I can tell, are forms that have the same shape, like a bun 'n burger. It hardly matters. "Muzak," the good doctor of industrial psychology continued, "helps human communities because it is a nonverbal symbolism for the common stuff of everyday living in the global village. And," he sped on, "Muzak promotes the sharing of meaning because it massifies symbolism in which not few, but all, can participate."

If Muzak is in the global village, I'm getting out and trying the global city. If they have it there as well, the global wilderness beckons. As for massifying symbolism, I don't know what it means, if anything, but my instinct tells me to be against it. I suspect, however, that mine is a losing cause. Consider the words of the director of music programming and recording for Muzak: "Our music is classified by a system of stimulus progression—some is more stimulating, some less. We put together 15-minute segments with the maximum stimulus in the last part of the segment." She has also said, "We at Muzak avoid using ˙. . . any . . . kind of music for the purposes of entertainment. Ours is functional music, sonorous design to humanize man-made environments."

Muzak does indeed avoid using music for entertainment. On the other hand, a man-made environment is by definition human; you cannot humanize it. But that is by the way. The term sonorous design is used to describe noise imposed on people for reasons of profit. This is public relations language, with a touch of social science, transcendent. Like acoustical perfume, it is a concept.

Concepts must be fought with concepts, which can be messy, but then war is a dirty business, and it is a military axiom that new weapons bring forth counterweapons. If you place something that blocks noise between the noise and you, you are employing a concept known as decibel buffering. If somebody could devise a portable decibel buffer (to be marketed commercially as Porta-buff) that could be pointed in the direction of the Muzak, the target of sonorous design would have a fair chance. I would never go out without one.

One night in January 1976 I was surrounded by conceptual-izers, though I did not fully understand the significance of concepts at the time. It was at a dinner marking the thirtieth anniversary of *PR News,* at which I delivered—here I had no quarrel with the press release—a witty talk on public relations parlance. For the occasion, I looked at the language of *PR News* itself and found it to be almost impeccable. Almost, so that my examination was only slightly, to use the language of *PR News,* resultful. That did not augur—in *PR News* it was spelled a-u-g-e-r, which is a tool for boring holes in wood—that did not augur well for my speech. But I did find in *PR News* a report of a conference that had been provocatively themed; it was devoted to issue solving. Issues may be resolved; they cannot be solved. Somebody at the provocatively themed conference was reported as having "reminded that 'we must communicate truthfully and continuously.'" I would like an occasional respite from communication so that it is not continu-ous. I would also like reminded to be followed by an object.

As it happened, I ran across a provocatively themed press release from the Chilton Book Company, of Radnor, Pennsylvania, publishers of a book, *Shake Down the Thunder!*, about Frank Leahy, the late football coach at Notre Dame. In the release Leahy was referred to as The Coach—upper case—and the other coaches as the other coaches—lower case. After suggesting that if the Roman Catholic Church were ever to create a Saint of the Gridiron—upper case again—it was likely to be Leahy, the release went on: "He brought more honor than a mortal should bring to football and Notre Dame." How much honor should a mortal bring to football and Notre Dame? Alas, there was no answer. Still, I was glad to have seen the press release for *Shake Down the Thunder!* Before I saw it I thought that The Coach was not Frank Leahy but The Head Coach in the Sky, who decides who wins, loses, and ties on Saturday afternoons.

A provocatively topicked release came from the publishing house of E. P. Dutton. It was written on behalf of a book about the American economy, and the headline read: *"Powerful new financial colossus foreseen."* Between the headline and the lead, somebody must have told the author of the press release that a colossus was, at the least, likely to be powerful. She shifted ground. The American economy, she wrote, will soon be dominated by a giant colossus, a giant colossus being different from a medium-sized colossus, and still more from the colossus that is a thirty-four short.

My employer engages in public relations, sometimes with provocative results. One NBC press release about a dramatization of *Robinson Crusoe* summarized the plot for those not familiar with it: "It focuses on Robinson Crusoe, of a middle class English family, who turns away from a chance to lead a relatively quiet life in England as a businessman in order to become a sailor. His days on the high seas end when his ship breaks apart on a reef off the coast of South America. That's when his greatest adventures begin, first as a man with a friend—a native he saved from certain death and named Friday."

There was hardly any need for the dramatization after that, though I may have assumed too much knowledge of the book.

WVUE-TV in New Orleans, Channel 8, advertised "a strange and eerie adventure on a hostile planet," which was the movie *Robinson Caruso on Mars*. Singing his heart out. Still, I wanted to watch Crusoe saving Friday from certain death. It is the most extreme kind of death one can be saved from.

*PR News*, it seemed to me, was not provocatively themed itself when it told of the prestigious PR Professional-of-the-Year Award. Awards that are not prestigious or at least coveted are rejected out of hand by those selected to receive them. There was a time when prestigious awards meant a great deal. I knew a man who had received the prestigious Emmy Award and the prestigious Overseas Press Club Award and the prestigious Peabody Award. He had not received the prestigious Du Pont Award, but all the same, on the strength of the three he had received, he was feeling his oats, a sexual perversion so rare that it has not yet been given a name, and he got into serious trouble because of it.

The reason prestigious awards have fallen in public esteem is that their winners are usually given only plaques, medals, or statuettes, which now seem relatively modest. When *Candide* was playing on Broadway, it was billed, with pride, as the "most admired and awarded musical." Clemson University, in South Carolina, points out in a leaflet that its library building has been "awarded for excellence in architectural design." Giving away hit shows and libraries is the sort of openhandedness one expects from Americans, but Clemson did not say to whom the library was awarded, and the producers of *Candide* did not specify the recipients, so the claims of both must be treated with reserve. Talk is cheap.

What else had I to complain about in *PR News*? There was a reference to a meeting in Nairobi of African mediamen. That would make me a North American mediaman. I didn't like the sound of it.

"Hello there, North American mediaman. What are you up to these days?"

"Trying to raise some money, sir. Can you help?"

"You know the old saying, my boy."

"What saying, sir?"

"Media borrower nor lender be." (Exits, humming "Media Me Tonight in Dreamland.")

There are few words more annoying than media. I entered the news business thirty-five years ago, and at the proper time I would like to leave it. I do not want to make my exit from the media. Others may. I do not. Calling the news business the media is a concept. There is enough of that sort of thing at large without people in news contributing to it.

I was suffering from pronounced ennui (pronounced onwee') one day in the recent past—June 9, 1975, to be precise—but it passed so quickly that I did not have time enough to report it to the Smithsonian Institution's Center for Short-Lived Phenomena. (If you want more information, the address is 60 Garden Street, Cambridge, Massachusetts 02138, but hurry. If you have trouble with delivery, you may be able to get help from the Institute for Democratic Communication, at the School of Public Communication, Boston University, 640 Commonwealth Avenue, Boston, Massachusetts 02215. If you'd rather do it yourself, the Institute for Local Self-Reliance, 1717 Eighteenth Street, Washington, D.C. 20009, can advise you; so can Action for Independent Maturity, Fulfillment Department, P.O. Box 2400, Long Beach, California 90801, and so can the Self-Help Institute of the Center for Urban Affairs at Northwestern University, Evanston, Illinois 60201. If you would like to be joined by others without regard to race, creed, or color, apply to the Center for the Study of American Pluralism, University of Chicago, 6030 South Ellis Avenue, Chicago, Illinois 60637. If you can't make up your mind how to proceed, try the Institute for Mediation and Conflict Resolution, at Automation House, 49 East Sixty-eighth Street, New York, N.Y. 10021.) What brought on the ennui was a news conference held by President Ford. Not that I expect presidential news conferences or gubernatorial news conferences, held by gubernators, or conferences held by those who have won what has become known as the mayorality, to be scintillating bits of entertainment. That is not what news conferences are for. They are part of the interface process, which reaches its ultimate expression when all parties turn the other cheek.

At the news conference Ford was asked whether he would run for the presidency in November 1976. He replied, "There is no doubt of my intention to run," which made it sound as though he had sat himself down before going out to meet the reporters and asked himself what his frame of mind was. What happened next seemed to me more characteristic of the media than of the news business. "Are you getting closer to a specific announcement?" a mediaman asked. The answer to that could hardly have been no, since American elections fall on fixed dates and Ford had already said that he would run. The President replied, "We are getting closer and closer to an announcement." The reporter, who before the answer may have thought that Ford could make time stand still, desisted. He had his story. And what a story: The President acknowledged that he was getting closer to an announcement. All concerned had interfaced.

Ford is not alone, of course, in playing these games. Many politicians announce that on such-and-such a date they will make an announcement. That gives them two news stories, plus speculation about what their announcement will be. Sometimes they announce that on such-and-such a date they will announce the date on which they will make an announcement. That gives them three stories, plus the speculation. President Ford, though he did not use the White House as a bully pulpit, which is nondenominational and suitable for clergymen who are overbearing, got more than that.

In politics, some of those doing public relations work are now known as media consultants, meaning that they tell the candidates how to deal with mediamen and mediawomen and the precious media they guard. One such, Tony Schwartz, a New York advertising man, has said that the best political commercials do not tell the viewer anything but rather "surface his feelings and provide a context for him to express those feelings." According to Schwartz, this invites the viewer to take part by providing meaning for the advertisement out of his own experience and emotions, and so is not manipulation but partipulation.

"Where have you been, dear?"

"At the media stand, buying a paper."

"Where are you now?"

"In what was formerly the recreation room, rumpus room, and family room, now known as the media room."

"What are you doing?"

"Watching television."

"What is it?"

"A commercial for Mo Udall."

"Have any feelings surfaced?"

"He makes me uncomfortable. I think he's partipulative. He won't get my vote."

Being in the media has, for some newsmen, the virtue of sounding more scientific and more technical, pulling them out of radio and television and into the electronic media, where they become electronic journalists. For the same reason a newsman may avoid the word expertness in his copy, preferring expertise, and, when entering a foreign country and being asked the purpose of his visit, reply reportage. I have used both myself, expertise not in years, but reportage as recently as September 1975, when I was sent to Tokyo to interview Emperor Hirohito before his visit to the United States. It was the first news interview the Emperor had ever granted, and while he did not say anything memorable—constitutional monarchs should not—I thought it no small thing to be taken to the room where the interview was to take place by the palace master of ceremonies and to be handed over, for the journey across the room to the Emperor, by the grand master of ceremonies. I had arrived in Tokyo without a visa, and at the airport, filling out a form that asked my business in Japan, I wrote reportage. I thought it sounded important and might help to get me through. As things worked out, I had to write a short biography of myself, explain why I had no visa—thoughtlessness was the answer—and promise in writing never to do it again. I should have been asked to promise never to say reportage again.

I do promise never to say media, except as the plural of medium, because, for our purposes, media conveys nothing; on the contrary, it conceals and misleads. There are, after all, many kinds of media. Money is a medium. Language is a medium. By themselves they are inert. Money makes no decisions of its own, nor does language. News is an active business in which news organizations compete with each other and every news item competes with every other item to get into print or on the air. Those in the business make decisions constantly, and if they consist of nothing more than throwing press releases in the waste basket, that is still significant. Most press releases are thrown away. Media would not do that. They would transmit them. Beyond this, all news organizations are not equally reliable, competent, enterprising, or unbiased. Even within individual news organizations— NBC, for example—the work is not uniform. All this the term media obscures. The American people ought to understand this in their own interest. If they did, they would have fewer illusions about what we do, fewer groundless expectations, and fewer disappointments. They would be better able to judge what we give them, and they might demand a better job from us, and get it.

Competition in news isn't only trying to get a story first. It may be getting a story nobody else has. It may be interpreting a story more intelligently or provocatively. It may be writing it more clearly or more sharply or more amusingly. Early in 1946 I was a member of the Washington bureau of the United Press and was assigned to cover the State Department. One day the second in command of the bureau, Julius Frandsen, said to me, not without kindness, "I never want to see indicate in a lead again." Indicate is a weak word. It has no place in a lead, but it is the sort of word you find yourself using almost automatically when you cover the State Department: "Secretary of State Dean Acheson indicated today that the United States was considering . . ." It has to be guarded against. Frandsen, the calmest, most deliberate, and, in consequence, one of the fastest newsmen I have ever known, did not want weak leads going out on the UP wire. That would only have meant, for papers taking both the UP and AP services, that the AP story would have the better chance of being printed. The competition is real and it is earnest. On September 27, 1974, the AP led a story this way: "Washington—A Senate Appropriations subcommittee has acted to ensure that former President Richard M. Nixon is not provided household servants at government expense." This was UPI's lead on the same story: "Washington— The chairman of a Senate subcommittee says the government shouldn't pay for shining Richard Nixon's shoes."

Victory tends to go to the wire service with the stronger, or catchier, lead. People who read the news, or listen to it, or watch it, ought to know that so that they can, when necessary, discount some part of what they are told. Calling news organizations media, which carries no hint of competition, does not help them to know it.

Competition on television may take other forms—who has the better pictures, the more appealing anchormen and anchorwomen, the snappier gimmicks, the more attractive set, the more striking visual effects, even whose weatherman grins more bravely at the lame jokes that suggest that he is responsible for the weather rather than for transmitting the government's forecast. Some of this is bunk, and television has few sights to offer more painful than the local anchorman taunting the sports broadcaster because one of his predictions went wrong ("You didn't look so good on that one, Al") or smiling determinedly and congratulating him because one came out right ("And here's our fearless forecaster, who was right on the nose again"), but it does not make news any less a business. It merely shifts the competition away from the news itself. It is true, of course, that the weatherman, who merely transmits a forecast others made, is a medium. So are television news broadcasters who do not write their own copy, who read whatever is put in front of them, and who bring no independent judgment to what they do. I think it is significant that publicity stunts and staged incidents are dismissed as media events. Nothing is dismissed by being called a news event.

News itself is competitive. What is news at nine o'clock in the morning may not be one or two minutes later. You can go into a studio to do a news show and, in the few minutes before going on the air, change the script because of breaking news—change stories, eliminate stories, add others. On a program like NBC

Nightly News, with a tight routine, with film and tape set to roll, commercials fixed, camera moves planned, and complex timing, a decision by the producer to change the show while on the air makes great demands not only of the broadcaster, who is out front where he can be seen, but of many people behind the scenes.

News is also an accidental business. Not always, of course; you can foresee some of what is coming, and one NBC News executive made himself famous by saying of a presidential inauguration parade, "I believe that this is what may be called a predictable event." Nobody was putting anything over on him. A good assignment editor, looking ahead, makes news as predictable as he can. To the extent that this can be done, news resembles public relations and advertising, in which effects are calculated and campaigns staged. But for those who are in it—perhaps I should speak only for myself—news is at its best when it is most accidental, for that is when it is most challenging. I don't have the same feeling walking to the studio to a daily television news program that I did when running to the studio to interrupt the broadcast of the 1973 World Series to announce that Spiro Agnew had resigned as Vice President or when it fell to me to announce on NBC radio that President Kennedy had been shot in Dallas. Even on a horrifying story—the murder of President Kennedy, the murder of Martin Luther King, Jr.—there is satisfaction in doing it well. Perhaps there is more satisfaction than comes from other stories, because the story is more important, and it is important that it be told accurately and without theatrics. This is nothing we choose, but for a newsman or newswoman, what is tragic or sad almost certainly provides better opportunities for demonstrating ability than happy events do. That is one thing that differentiates news from public relations and advertising. Public relations usually, and advertising always, tries to create expectations of happiness.

On the last night of the 1964 Democratic convention, in Atlantic City, New Jersey, President Johnson was speaking. It was the climax of the affair, the king acknowledging the affection of his people. I was on the floor of the convention hall, standing near some members of the Mississippi Freedom Party delegation. They, blacks and whites, most of them poor, had come to Atlantic City to challenge the regular Mississippi delegation. A compromise had been worked out and some of them were seated. On the last night the entire delegation was on the floor. As President Johnson spoke about freedom and liberty, a black woman in the Freedom Party group began to cry. I told the NBC producer in charge of our coverage. Should he cut away from the President? If he did, why to this one person out of the thousands in the hall? Again, if he did, what did it show—that she was weeping for what she knew about the United States, or the President, or the Democratic Party, or Mississippi? Or was she simply overwhelmed by being where she was?

There was little time to think, and there was no textbook, or study of the "media," setting out what should be done. News judgment is an amalgam of experience, knowledge, wisdom, workmanship, and competitive urge. His amalgam told the NBC producer to cut to the woman. I hope we will never get to the day when that is called media judgment.

During the Viet Cong and North Vietnamese Tet offensive in 1968, some unusual film came into NBC. (The Associated Press also had stills of it.) It showed a man, dressed in shorts and a sport shirt and identified as a Viet Cong, being taken along a street in Saigon to the chief of the South Vietnamese national police. The police chief, without a word, drew a revolver, put it to the man's head, and shot him dead. Somebody at NBC had to decide what to do with that film. If you use it, are you implying that this kind of thing is going on wholesale? Suggesting that there should be sympathy for the unarmed underdog shot down in cold blood? How much do you show? The look on the doomed man's face as he realizes what is about to happen? His face as the bullet strikes? His head hitting the pavement, the blood running out of his head, the blood running down the gutter? Where do you cut off? The decisions are made according to the news judgment of the person, or persons, making them. That is circular: those who decide decide. But that is the way it happens.

A few weeks after the Tet offensive, President Johnson decided not to run again. A medium would simply have transmitted what he said, which was that he was stepping aside to demonstrate the genuineness of his desire for peace in Vietnam, to show that his offer to negotiate was not being made for political advantage. As a journalist, I had an obligation to point out that Johnson had barely beaten Eugene McCarthy in the New Hampshire primary a few weeks earlier, that he was evidently about to lose to McCarthy in Wisconsin, that Robert Kennedy had entered the contest for the nomination, that Johnson could not go anywhere in the country except to military bases without hostile demonstrations, and much more. Nor would a medium have been in the fix that I was in that night. We had been given an advance copy of the speech with the warning that the President would say something that was not in the text. We were led to believe that he would announce a trip. He was almost at the end of the prepared text when I realized that he was about to announce his withdrawal from politics. The director, who was not listening, began to remind me, through the listening device in my ear—it's called a Telex—how long I would speak, where we'd switch to when the speech was over, that sort of thing.

I was trying to take notes on what the President was saying, also coming to me on the Telex, drawing my hand across my throat as a signal for silence and trying to convey by grimacing and by clutching my head that the stage manager and cameramen should tell the director to be quiet. I was also shouting, "Shut up!" into my microphone, which made three voices talking at once. Eventually the director was prevailed upon by the producer to stop talking, and later he performed heroically in improvising the changes that had to be made. Directors often do perform miracles, but they don't always listen. At the 1964 Democratic convention in Atlantic City I was covering the announcement by the credentials committee of its decision in the seating of delegates from Mississippi. I was to broadcast from the room where the announcement was being made. As it began, the director came through on the Telex with a reminder of the time allotted me, switch cues, and so on.

"Don't talk to me now," I said into my microphone, trying to hear the announcement.

He went on.

"Don't talk to me now," I said again. I said it a number of times.

Governor David Lawrence of Pennsylvania, the committee chairman, grew tired of the competition. He looked down at me. "Tell them," he said, "that I agree with you."

It was not one of my happiest moments, but these are small things. News is a great business. I count myself lucky to be in it. My vendetta against the term media arises not only for the reasons already given but because it implies a go-between, one who takes orders and carries messages, one who is employed by others for their purposes. There is no suggestion of the quality we need most, which is independence.

When I hear somebody say media, I think of a phrase heard long ago from somebody whose English was ungrammatical but eloquent: "I ain' in dat." My difficulty arises from the fact that so many people won't believe that I ain'.

Independence may be a prerequisite of the news business, but public relations and advertising encourage a cheerful dependency. In the glamorous life I lead, public relations persons are always ready to do my bidding. Three spades, they will cry out for me, and four diamonds, and, on occasion, he passes. They ply me with gifts, both free gifts of the sort offered by savings banks to new depositors, and the other kind. I still have to buy some things for myself, however, and here I am much affected by advertising. I try to do as I am told. For example, I like what I wear to communicate my personal fashion statement, direct, definitive, and pertinent, and the result is that I buy my clothes where European influences are adapted for the American man of status, with an ultimate sense of quality and understated elegance, expressed in a peak lapel, deep center vent, suppressed waist, and higher armholes. My waist sometimes demands freedom of expression, but what is made for me there is styled to underscore my élan and to project my personality—which varies, with my ties reflecting the variations: adventurous plaids when I am adventurous, discreet patterns when I am discreet. Even the fabrics are au courant. The fall scenario calls for young wools, and later, when the weather is colder, much of what I wear is fur-lavished. Some of my other costumes are buttery-soft leathers that are an extension of my own body, which is buttery soft itself. Saks Fifth Avenue, for one, sells a magnificient—m-a-g-n-i-f-i-c-i-e-n-t—glacé leather trench coat collared and lined with natural muskrat. Unnatural muskrat is a muskrat of doubtful sexual proclivities and would not be welcome on any coat of mine.

When riding the seven-ten to the Hamptons, or holding forth in the board room, I wear clothes cut to cope with a man's pace, and with that certain offhand sense of style and nonchalance that lets me know I've arrived. Sometimes they let me know I've arrived before the train is at the Hamptons, but I've learned not to get off without looking at the station's name, or at my wrist watch, which is united with its bracelet in an unbroken contemporary line and gives me the kind of timekeeping dependability that inspires my eternal loyalty. My luggage, which confers quality status, contains a wraparound that is a long drink of stretch terry to soak up the sea après swim.

It is a heady life. Gifts I buy at Tiffany's; where else would one find whisperweight earrings designed to go into one pierced ear and out the other? Used cars I do not drive. I do not even drive cars that have seen prior service. Nor, among new cars, will I settle for one of Detroit's mass-produced status symbols. I insist on a personal statement of automotive comfort, the epitome of automotive elegance, a luxury performance car at a realistic price, made with unhurried European craftsmanship, with rack-and-pinion steering and a negative steering-roll radius, and powered by a highly responsive four-cylinder, twin overhead cam engine that is coupled to a five-speed overdrive transmission. I regard the coupling of the four-cylinder engine and the five-speed transmission as indispensable. It is, moreover, a thing of beauty. You can watch it without feeling that you are a voyeur at all.

About my apartment this has been said: "The overall grandeur of this space is memorably enticing. The magnanimity of leasehold improvements is so well-designed, it would likely appeal to anyone." I cannot speak for anyone else, but well-designed magnanimity has always appealed to me, especially since it became tax deductible.

In the luminous retreat that is my apartment, the bedrooms are filled with what I am assured is Old World charm, despite the fact that the curtains are made of a Redi-Prest blend of dacron polyester and rayon, and the multicolored comforter fluffed with lightweight polyester fiberfill. There is also New World charm, thanks to new concept furniture, fabrics, and wallpaper. Life without concepts, as we well know, would be empty. Sheets and pillowcases I have drawn from the Mixed Emotions collection, a responsive range of coordinated bed and bath fashions that differ in mood from pattern to pattern and from color to color and yet intermingle beautifully, with an impact that can be serene or startling. My preference is for the unexpected. It sets off my casually cool and tasteful pajamas.

The bathrooms have finely crafted switch plates, door pulls, and towel bars that offer charisma for the commonplace. In the reception rooms the high-pile texturizing of the carpeting gives special shadings and diffuses footprints (which has proved to be a mixed blessing). The silver is in an elegant, tastefully restrained pattern that gracefully complements both formal and informal appointments. The kitchen has been described as the gourmetest in town, and because it is, I once opened there a packet of gourmet couscous manufactured by the Ferrero Company of Vitrolles, Bouches-du-Rhône (Mouths-of-the-Rhône), which exports to the United States Le Vrai Couscous Extra (the Real Couscous Out of the Ordinary). You may want to know how the broth for the couscous is prepared:

"Take a nice chicken or a little bit of mutton, or still better the two sorts of meat together, cut it into pieces and parboil it. Put it into your pot with the necessary water. Salt and join hot pepper (the pungent sauce with red pimento, grinded in a cup, can be served separately), join the chick-peas, a tuft of pot-herbs, onion, garlick (if you desire), and all possible vegetable according to the seasons.

"The broth must be very perfumed and can be favoured with spices. Pour the cooked couscous into a deep plate, undo the balls, which eventually could have been occured, in stiring with fresh butter. Serve the couscous, vegetable and meat, broth, in 3 different plates. Each companion will accomodate the couscous according to his taste, i.e. more or less of the broth and of the pungent sauce, as well as the vegetable of his choice."

I joined the chick-peas, was occured, and have not been the same since.

I drink a gin that is the quintessence of an exceptionally well-mannered martini ("Not too cold for you, sir, I hope," I have heard it say) and occasionally shift to a happy vodka, which may burst into song on the way down, but with a limited repertoire because Russian songs tend to be moody—"None But the Lonely Heart," "The Volga Boatman," and that sort of thing. Usually the vodka manages only Moussorgsky's "Song of the Flea," and I am growing tired of its great peals of bass-baritone laughter. My liqueur hails from the land where love comes first and the liqueur comes second. It is appreciated for its glowing color and a flavor that is, quite frankly, romantic.

I don't smoke. However, some of my friends will not entertain the idea of giving up cigarettes because they have found smoking a cigarette to be a rare and pleasurable private moment. Some smoke a cigarette with a filter based on a new design concept; for others the cigarette is a proud smoke, boastful even. But now and then all shift to a cigarette with a long, lean, all-white dynamite look (their hands tremble when they light up). A few use a cigarette that is alive with pleasure, and the fact that if they continue smoking it may still be alive with pleasure when they are not bothers them not at all.

Living in a total concept of leisure calls for little outside entertainment, and I confine my moviegoing to major motion pictures, though I notice that lately there are few of any other kind. I see some major motion pictures on the television sets in hotel rooms. On one trip alone I saw a major motion picture (it was actually a Major Motion Picture) about the wicked, wacky thirties, one that told The Story of a Girl's Love, a Boy's Courage and a Rogue's Reckless Daring, and one in which Sinbad battled the creatures of legend in the miracle of Dynarama. Dynaramite! After a while you can spot major motion pictures as quickly as Hollywood does. Harold Robbins's *The Pirate* could hardly help becoming a major motion picture since it was, according to its publisher, Simon and Schuster (a richly edited house), "richly charactered." This brought the producer requests for jobs from many character actors, including one who had played the part of engine corrosion in an antifreeze commercial.

When I read, I find myself drawn to a magazine that is a brand-new media option for advertisers, with a unique new up-scale audience mix made up of magazine imperatives, who account for 43.6 per cent of the new cars purchased by men, 53.5 per cent of the radial tires, and 53.5 per cent of the air trips. Some of the magazine imperatives apparently have radial tires but not cars, but it is a group I feel I should be identified with. With books, I tend to wait for such events as the publication of the Avon spectacular, Joyce Verrette's *Dawn of Desire,* which received major advertising and promotion featuring floor displays plus a media mix of major TV, buses, newspapers, and magazines, which is only right for a blazing, tumultuous novel of a love as old as time, as timeless as forever. Still, I am broad-minded and will also read a book that is destined to become a classic. There are not many of these.

Tennis is a passion of mine. I step onto the court, clad in a red-and-green-striped white cotton tennis shirt. My shorts are the same colors, with terry side panels. After my victory I slip into my color-coordinated sweater and shake my good-sport-coordinated opponent's hand.

Women? Here it is simply a matter of what happens in a setting of overall grandeur and an exciting lifestyle. The grandeur and excitement attract women who use cosmetics that give off a deep, throaty purr of luxury. This means, to begin with, a fragrance evoking a season of lilacs and plums, the vigor of cypress, the charm of amber, lingering, opulent, and stunning, and that says exactly what the woman wearing it wants it to say, unless, of course, she wants it to tell a man to go away, which perfumes do not regard as their mission and find it difficult to do. Alternatively, it may mean a perfume that has little, light oriental tones (for mystery), new floral blends (for youth), and what professional perfumers call green notes (for sparkle), resulting in a scent that whispers, "This woman is sure of herself yet mysterious, sophisticated but young and sparkling."

It's an odd effect, a woman standing there, her lips brushed with extraordinary gel lipgloss, which gives them sheer, glistening color, her superluscious creme eyeshadow in a long-lasting, non-creasing color, and her nails like iced porcelain thanks to a two-phase color-coordinated system that adds a new, highly reflective quality to perfect frosts, her makeup an extraordinary coup for skin with both oily and drier areas because it blots and moisturizes at the same time, while from her come fairly complicated whispered messages. Those hearing them for the first time may be upset, and the hard of hearing often ask for a repeat: "What's that again? I didn't quite get what you said." It's a sure party pickup.

Such a woman knows that for the admiration she thrives on she needs in-depth skin care with an extract in which natural ingredients and soluble proteins blend to make her skin look young and resilient. The extract goes on under moisturizer and makeup and accompanies her on her travels, though the purring cosmetics sometimes do not. The airlines have asked her not to transmit while in the air. On her legs she wears Frivole, the pantystocking with the high-rise panty top on a sheer stocking, ideal for wear in a high-rise building. When she walks, her feet are encased in trendy wedges, in which a classic moc-toe is deftly outlined with fine stitches and punctuated with a goldtone ornament. Or she may wear a quintessential dress moc with a welted front porch and heels stocked knee-high to a grasshopper. She may also be shod in burnished brown and lickety licorice black consummate spring walkers replete with all the newsworthy blandishments, among them high points traced with moccasin welting, contrast stitchery, and gilting here and there.

She is an American woman in the Bicentennial era. And the only revolution going on is in her head. It starts with a concept. Of luxe. And luxe is what she's always yearned for. No one can dictate fashion to her any more. There are no more absolutes. In the spring she welcomes the dash of pantsuiting that explores all possibilities, and a crisp butcher's coat that wraps over slacks expresses her adventurous attitude and shares her limitless potential. When she likes to feel utterly original a dash of silk chiffon makes her evenings sing, and if the chiffon is set afire with yellow and orange tiger lilies in a bed of reeds on a beige ground, she will be both tigress and temptress. To prepare for the beach, where the summer/she is the most sensuous creature under the sun, jeweled with stones and shells, she uses a soap that won't de-fat, deterge, or denature the skin, thanks to its mild heavy-molecular triethanolamine-base formulation.

I am as grateful to heavy molecules as the summer/she is. It is not generally understood how these stable configurations of atomic nuclei and electrons remain bound together by electromagnetic forces. It is an accomplishment taken altogether too much for granted. Also, a skin without terge is a horrible sight, and we can all be glad that we are spared having to see it.

# 6

# Paradigm Lost

I know of a condominium in Pompano Beach, Florida, which in the plans given to prospective buyers identifies the kitchen as a culinary center, the bedroom as a sleeping chamber, and the dining room as a place de dinner. La Plage Pompano would have been an appropriate setting for a dish served to me and others in the Athens of America at a book-and-author luncheon sponsored by the *Boston Herald*: Crepes à la sea food. Both the *Herald* and the condominium may have acted on the basis of technical advice from the Biltmore Hotel in New York City, where, for the benefit of visitors drifting over from the United Nations, a sign outside a men's lavatory announces not only Gentlemen but Monsieurs.

The Culinary Institute of America, in Hyde Park, New York, is also a place de dinner of sorts. It was founded in 1946 "to provide educational opportunities for individuals seeking success-ful and rewarding careers in food service hospitality." Those seeking unsuccessful and unrewarding careers evidently are encouraged to look elsewhere. The Institute has a Rabelais Grill with a different grill-type menu, and an Escoffier Restaurant which, by deduction, must have a restaurant-type menu that the grill-type menu is different from. Those who want to make reservations are invited to use a Maitre d' Tel Hot Line. The Maitre probably can tell you what the soup d' jour is and assign you to a t' ble, but you do not ask him for a d' ble room. That might annoy him and might make L' Institut a crisis-type setting. Not everybody is at his best in that kind of setting, but George Washington was at Valley Forge, and so was William M. Birenbaum. In the spring of 1976 Birenbaum was chosen by the search committee looking for a new president for Antioch College, Yellow Springs, Ohio. Inez Smith Reid, professor of political science at Barnard College, in New York City, was chairwoman of the committee. Birenbaum, she explained, was "a populist-type leader" and an "experienced chief executive with a strong track record in crisis-type settings."

When Washington ran the revolutionary-type war that made the country independent, compiling a strong track record may have been easier. The country did not yet have what Jimmy Carter has called a heterogeneous-type American population. Nonetheless, I have always had the average amount of respect for Washington, first President, first in war, first in peace, first in the hearts of his countrymen, and, according to Byron, Cincinnatus of the West. Some small flaws, no doubt, but who, Mesdames and Monsieurs, is without them? It was not until the nation reached its Bicentennial that I learned that there was more wrong with George Washington than most of us realized. The diagnosis was made by Louis G. Heller, professor of classical languages and Hebrew at City College of New York, and James Macris, professor of English and linguistics at Clark University, Worcester, Massachusetts. The father of his country stood in need of massive remediation. He was weak in punctuation and spelling.

Remediation appeals to those in education for the same reason that a place de dinner appeals to condominium promoters in Florida. An unnecessary abstruseness is introduced, a hint of complexity. There is a suggestion that what is being discussed is, in the case of remediation, beyond the understanding of most, and in the case of the place de dinner, beyond their pocketbooks. For remediators and developers of places de dinner, substituting the soft and the bloated for the concrete and specific makes the heart beat faster. It is a declaration of importance and is increasingly characteristic of life in the United States, where fringe benefits become collateral entitlements and toilets personal convenience rooms, where children in school are told not to ask to leave the room but to request a health break, and where an excuse becomes first a rationalization and then a legitimizing tactic.

Aboard an American Airlines flight from New York to Los Angeles, a stewardess asked, "For your meal preference, would you like beef Stroganoff, chicken, or fruit plate?" I had already had a large preference, and abstained. Frontier Airlines, which surely used to offer free soft drinks, now offers complimentary soft beverages. This is hardly the language of the frontier:

"What'll it be, pardner?"

"Make mine a soft beverage. No chaser."

When I lived in Britain in the 1950s, somebody in the Labour government came up with the phrase (he probably did not realize that it was a concept*) parity of esteem. He wanted graduates of technical schools to enjoy parity of esteem with university graduates. They did not then and do not now, and it is easy to see why. What teacher would want to teach children when he could remediate them massively instead?† It is as unlikely as somebody volunteering to his quietus make with a bare bodkin.

---

* See Chapter 5.

† The director of the Field Services Division of the New Jersey Department of Education, Catherine Kavrilesky, has said that teachers will be held responsible for any students who cannot read. "If we go into a school district and find a teacher who has a classroom filled with kids who can't read, we are going to expect to find the reason," Ms. Kavrilesky said. "If the reason is incompetence, we expect that teacher to undergo remediation, and if remediation fails, we expect to see that teacher dismissed, tenure or not." Remediation, if it means anything, means applying a remedy. Remedies cannot fail. Or could not, before American educators got hold of them.

There has to be some explanation for the fact that, as we become more and more open about ourselves, speak ever more freely about sex, see homosexuality come out of the closet and homosexuals become a public pressure group, demand and get more and more intimate information about our politicians, and—men and women alike—use language in what once would have been called polite society that no polite society would tolerate, our language in other parts of our lives becomes less and less frank, more and more covered and obscure. Both developments have the same source and the same purpose. We are calling attention to ourselves, in the one case with arresting four-letter words (which soon cease to be arresting because of overuse) and in the other with pumped-up job descriptions and titles.

I once used the term "garbageman" in a broadcast. It was at the time of the strike by garbage collectors in Memphis, Tennessee, in 1968, in the course of which Martin Luther King, Jr., was killed. I soon received a letter from a woman who told me that her husband was one of the men I had referred to. "My husband is not garbage," she wrote. "Please don't call him that again." I wrote back saying that no such thought was intended, and I did not use the term again. The point, though—which I had the good sense not to offer the woman who wrote to me—is that respect should not come from titles. It should come from an understanding of the work being done and the value of the person doing it. It should come from reality, not from camouflage.

We should not, for example, scorn those who collect and dispose of our garbage. We should be grateful to them. Our cities would not be habitable without them. We could have less garbage for them to dispose of if we reduced "packaging," but that seems to be beyond us. Indeed, instead of cutting down the packaging of things, we have taken to packaging ideas. We even package the absence of ideas, emptiness. It gets the gaudiest packages of all.

Remediation is, as these things go, a package of moderate size. The first time I ran across it, it took me some time to realize that it had nothing to do with mediating, still less with mediating again. It appeared in the November 1974 issue of *Change,* an education magazine, which contained an article by David L. Kirp and Mark G. Yudof about admission quotas for students in colleges, universities, and graduate schools. While discussing "the task of making up for past discrimination," Kirp and Yudof wrote this: "In many cases, the burden of remediation to overcome past deficiencies is staggering." Kirp and Yudof could have spoken of the burden of remedying past deficiencies. They did not have to use remedy in any form: In many cases, the burden of overcoming past deficiencies is staggering. Educators prefer to remediate. Charles G. Walcutt, graduate professor of English at the City University of New York, wrote, "The colleges, trying to remediate increasing numbers of . . . illiterates up to college levels, are being high-schoolized." High-schoolized colleges will need remediation themselves, or, getting into the spirit of the thing, remediational activities. This last phrase appeared in a letter from the Southeast Mental Health and Retardation Center in Fargo, North Dakota. Remediation-type activities will no doubt be next.

I should have been ready for remediation because, three months earlier, I had been introduced to reinforcer emission. This came about through an article, "Reinforcement Practices of Black and White Teachers in Integrated Classrooms," in the August 1974 (a vintage year in its way, 1974) issue of the *Journal of Educational Psychology*. Credulous fellow that I am, I thought it had something to do with teachers being held in strategic reserve to be dispatched from room to room to repel boarders. It had nothing to do with that. Instead, the teachers were reinforcing the children by a process of emission, and the study covered not only the number of reinforcers the teachers emitted but whether they tended to be of the traditional distant kind—promotion next term, or possibly skipping a grade—or proximity reinforcers such as material rewards and close personal contact.

In other words—and if only it were—the subject was how the teachers encouraged the children. The educational advantage in saying emitting reinforcers rather than encouraging children—or, for that matter, calling a teacher a facilitator or enabler, a teaching period a module, and a classroom a learning station—escapes me.

That there is an educational disadvantage does not. Stuffiness and fake erudition are being substituted for reality and clarity. No child goes home after school and tells her mother that during a module in the learning station that day the enabler emitted a reinforcer in her direction. "And it was a proximity reinforcer, too, Mommy!"

I remember a teacher in junior high school—an elderly, determined woman, Miss O'Connell—giving my hair a yank one day when I was disrespectful. This was not so much reinforcing as enforcing, but it fell into the proximity category. It kept me in order for the rest of the module.

The father of a child about to enter a junior high school in Los Angeles sent me a circular he had received from the school principal. It explained the seventh-grade curriculum and it contained this sentence: "We are planning an articulation visit to all our feeding elementary schools in the near future." He thought this meant that parents could talk to teachers.

When New York City was, in 1975, somewhat belatedly trying to remain solvent, the chancellor of the city's schools, Irving Anker, said, "I am reluctant to effectuate economies through the closing of schools, even for one day. I also have a question about the legality of such action." Anker could have said, "I hesitate to save money by closing schools. Also, it may be illegal." If he had, he might have lost his professional standing. He might, for example, have been shunned by the coordinator of research of the department of education of an eastern state who wrote to thank someone for sending him "summarizative descriptions of law and citizenship programs."

Despite his thanks, the research coordinator had some doubts about the worth of the law and citizenship materials in his dissemination program due to—he meant because of—their lack of evaluative data, and he was troubled by the fact that the programs would require as instructors professional law personnel—lawyers, one assumes. He thought that this would "serve to delimit the installation possibilities in a local education agency." I suppose he meant limit.

It is no joke when the coordinator of research in a state education department does not know the difference between limit, to confine or restrict, and delimit, to demarcate, to establish boundaries, but what is more important is that this language is repellent. I mean this literally: it will drive people away from education. The least harm it can do is put about the wrong idea of what eloquence and lucidity are.

What must conversation among these people be like?

"What are you up to these days, Anker?"

"I am effectuating economies. And you, research coordinator?"

"I am reading summarizative descriptions of law and citizenship programs, but I fear that they will not be suitable for a dissemination program because of their lack of evaluative data and their requirement of professional law personnel."

In 1974 a summer program of the New York City Board of Education became the subject of a report by the Youth Services Administration. The writer, possibly expecting his work to be seen by Irving Anker, warmed up by assuaging unforeseen difficulties and facilitating goals. He spoke of employees who had been robbed after drawing their pay checks, listed precautions that had been taken against this, and concluded, "These precautions appeared to be quite successful in dissuading potential individuals with larcenous intent." This is a new way of looking at the well-known occupational group, the perpetrators. Perpetrators are potential individuals who have not been dissuaded. Undissuaded, they perpetrate and run the risk of being observed ("I observed the perpetrator") and apprehended ("and apprehended same").

Dissuading potential individuals is more likely to succeed if it is begun early. The Community Health Care Center of the University of Minnesota asked for $35,000 from the Governor's Crime Commission to buy dogs: "The major objective of the project is to assess the extent to which early education via the use of pets, in empathy, responsibility, and regard for behavioral consequence are instrumental in deterring potentially delinquent

9-year-old boys from committing delinquent acts." If the project backfires, Minnesota may find itself facing not only the boys but an unusually large population of potentially delinquent dogs, leading in turn to more money for assessment, perhaps a deficit, a period of fiscal restraint, and a program of cost avoidance.

Recently, in New York, a policewoman dissuaded a potential individual by disarming and arresting him and breaking his nose when he resisted. The incident was investigated by police captain Irving Liebman, who said, "This is strictly a kosher case. There's absolutely nothing wrong with what she did."

Then the captain emitted a reinforcer: "The entire incident," he said, "was commendatory of female police officers." In fact, it wasn't. It may have spoken well of the policewoman, Arlene Egan, but told nothing about other policewomen, any more than an act of bravery by a policeman tells something about other policemen. Probably it was the climate of the times. Captain Liebman simply wanted to say commendatory. Kosher was better.

When Captain Liebman said commendatory, he was speaking one of the more exotic forms of education language, that of the honorary degree, which flowers every spring when heads of university honorary degree committees, with no apparent embarrassment, address to those receiving the degrees such reinforcers as these:

Like one of Horatio Alger's youthful heroes, your rise from obscurity to power has been swift.

You set an example not only for musicians in your devotion to the discipline of your craft, but for everyone with the vitality and harmony of your being.

You bind rifts in the fabric of your city, disproving Yeats's apocalyptic vision that the center cannot hold.

Not one to be awed into silent inactivity by the promises of pure technology, you have dealt with the implications of science with a calm logic and with consistent attention to its human role.

Your histrionic versatility is such that as an actress, in roles sometimes sophisticated or fiery, sometimes naïve or demure, your technical achievement cannot be categorized.

Those are the genuine article. Emboldened by such precedent Captain Liebman could have said to Arlene Egan: You have opened new paths for female police officers, and you have not flinched from danger. Your methods have been worthy of an ancient ethnic tradition.

Now for a thrust:

"The major thrust of Youth Services Agency's recommendations to maximize the quality and efficiency of services rendered revolve around the necessity for more phone channels. Two additional phone channels would compensate greatly for both communicative and space difficulties and such implementation is strongly urged as an immediate necessity."

Revolve should be revolves, and such implementation is also urged as an immediate necessity, but no matter. A revolving major thrust is hard to match. It is as rare in our part of the world as a whirling dervish. However, the nonrevolving species is spotted fairly often. It was seen at the 1975 convention of the American Booksellers Association, where a press release noted that the major thrust of the convention was to "foster dialogue." I had thought that it was to foster reading.

The report on the Board of Education program concluded with the Youth Services Agency's opinion that the program "should be considered for expanded allotments of enrollee personnel and more supportive measures from its own direct funding source." This is packaging again—the equivalent of wrapping paper, decorative tape and bows, boxes within boxes, tissue paper, all of it having to be peeled away and discarded to get at the recommendation of more workers and more money that lies within.

Major thrusts are fairly widely distributed in the New York City government. In the fiscal year ending in June 1974, 862,000 potholes were repaired, and although the number to be filled in the next fiscal year was about the same, one Budget Bureau official felt able to say that whereas "Potholes were a major thrust before" they were no longer, and it was time to look elsewhere for new productivity gains. The number of potholes does seem extraordinary; it might have been easier to drive the unpotholed parts of the streets down to pothole level rather than build the potholes up.

Two sources of strength of the United States are that it is large and has distinct regions. I was about to say that it is also varied, but it isn't. The educators, packaging relentlessly, make us all one. Where New York calls for supportive measures from direct funding sources, the Metro School Board of Nashville, Tennessee, discussing curriculum planning, states its intentions thus: "Programmatic assumptions will be specified, competencies identified, a rationale developed and instructional objectives stated. Pre-assessment, post-assessment, learning alternatives and remediation will be an integral part of instructional modules within the framework of program development."

Four hundred miles west, it is argued in a paper on "The Need for a University of Arkansas Continuing Education Center" that "the continuing education program should never be finalized. Rather, it should be a flexible, chameleon-like product, ever responding to the changing needs of the people of the State. However, broad programmatic thrusts might be articulated, thus providing parameters for decision-making and increasing the benefit yield." The need, changing or otherwise, of the people of Arkansas for a chameleon-like product of any kind may be doubted, and the belief that the articulation of broad programmatic thrusts provides (or emits) parameters for decision making ("Sir Gawain thrust his sword programmatically toward the villain, and as it caught the light it seemed to shower parameters on the loyal Arkansans, who were gathered expectantly near a backlog of decisions") is a delusion. Many a thrust has produced not a single parameter, for the reason that parameters are artful dodgers and refuse to be rounded up. The benefit yield is something else. It may well be increased by programmatic thrusting, but without the parameters who would want it?

It is not generally understood how elusive parameters are; nor is it understood that thrusts may be dangerous. I was in Madison, Wisconsin, in September 1974 and saw, in the local paper, the *State Journal,* an interview with the new dean of the Department of Home Economics of the University of Wisconsin, Elizabeth J. Simpson. (Not that it is called Home Economics any longer; it has become Family Resources and Consumer Sciences.) The dean was discussing her previous job, in the Office of Education in Washington, and she said that much of her recent work had been in "conceptualizing new thrusts in programming." The dean is a brave woman. Beware the conceptualized thrust. I saw one that had gone berserk and it took six strong men to hold it down.

The spirit that turns home economics into family resources and consumer sciences is everywhere. When the University of Miami had a deficit of $560,000, its president, Henry King Stanford, was undaunted.* "We will divert the force of this fiscal stress," Dr. Stanford said, "into leverage energy to pry improved budgetary prediction and control out of our fiscal and administrative procedures." Dr. Stanford meant that he intended to cut some

---

* He could, in the way of university presidents, as easily be Henry Stanford King, Stanford Henry King, Stanford King Henry, King Stanford Henry, or King Henry Stanford. There is a requirement, not statutory but widely acknowledged, that university presidents have interchangeable names, three if possible. This lends dignity to their institutions. Those who wish to pursue this matter further may consult my earlier work, *Strictly Speaking,* Bobbs-Merrill, New York 1974, pages 117–122. They will also find their own research rewarding. A New York lawyer has written to me that he saw a university presidency ahead for his grandson, MacLaren Marshall Richardson. Another lawyer, Spencer Agassiz Gard, of Iola, Kansas, wondered why he was not a university president. He may be certain that a university will be constructed around him before the decade is out. Lounsbury Danforth Bates, who also wrote, is the librarian of the Harvard Club in New York and not a university president. However, Bates is known as Biff, which may be the reason.

The ideal university president's interchangeable name was that of Nicholas Murray Butler, who was president of Columbia from 1902 to 1945. Among those I mentioned as following the Butler tradition was Forrest David Mathews of the University of Alabama. Mathews became Secretary of Health, Education and Welfare, and in May 1976 received from Columbia University the Nicholas Murray Butler award, in silver. Whether the award is given for something more than having a name like Nicholas Murray Butler's I do not know and I would like to think not, but by the time Mathews received it he was calling himself F. David Mathews. Not the same. Not the same at all.

costs. When Betty Friedan taught at Yale, the students complained that she lectured too much. Ms. Friedan declared herself open to change, whereupon, so one student put it, the seminar was "restructured toward interaction." He meant the students were allowed to talk more. Says a member of the Federal Communications Commission, a former law professor, about regulation of children's television: The First Amendment "does not mean that we can make judgments on the basis of majoritarian sentiments alone." Fair enough. The minoritarians have their rights too. The woman in charge of publications in a rehabilitation hospital in New York State ran across "fostering interfamilial meaningful relationships with counselees recovering from cardio-vascular-pulmonary malfunctions." She deduced that it meant counseling families of heart attack and stroke patients. Edith P. Lewis, editor of *Nursing Outlook,* passed along to me a sentence she received in the line of duty: "Finalization of the implementation of the program which, it had been decided by the faculty, would facilitate forward movement toward goal achievement was made operational in the penultimate semester." In American society the penultimate is mightier than the sword.

Not long ago an appeal for money reached me from an organization at Princeton University that was looking for viable solutions to the complex and pressing problems of peace. Without them, I was warned, our very survival will continue to be imperiled, which is logical: Them as ain't viable won't last long. The older generation does tend to live in the past, but we used to look for solutions to problems and were pleasantly surprised on the rare occasions when we found them. Solutions are no longer sufficient; viability is required. Viable has moved into the legal profession: "The consent under Section 341(f) might be a viable solution if the corporation was subject to the capital gain tax under Section 1378(c). However, the development of such a situation would be very likely to be unusual." That would make viability very likely to be unusual, as well.

And if not viability, effectiveness. A statement of policy from the Committee for Economic Development said that a new generation of complex problems demanded fresh and effective solutions. A solution not effective would not be a solution. Nor need a solution be fresh. Old solutions do the job, and have the advantage of experience.

I mentioned money two paragraphs above. In the context it seems rude. Among restructurers toward interaction and those who look for grants for technical training because "a quality void in technical capacity constrains achievement," money is too bald a word. They prefer funds, or better still funding, because it sounds like something continuing. Again, they would rather not say continuing. Ongoing is preferred.

Ongoing has a mesmerizing quality. City College of New York wanted to have a communications center which would "train students to work within their immediate communications environment" and would have an ongoing placement service. How that would differ from a placement service was not made clear. Perhaps a placement service finds jobs for its clients while an ongoing placement service finds jobs for those who have demonstrated sufficient motivation to achieve in an appropriate employment setting. (Hands across the border: the part of the last sentence that begins with "demonstrated sufficient motivation" drifted down with a cold air mass from Winnipeg, Canada.)

A preparatory school I know sends questionnaires to the parents of applicants. Why, one question goes, have you chosen us? One father replied, "We feel that [name of school] offers an optimal synthesis of the traditional education in the fundamentals of learning and innovative education in creative involvement." The parent who brought this forth probably had his child accepted with a scholarship and was himself invited to revise the school's catalogue.

In the field of education the competition in producing nonsense is intense. What does the scientific method in the social sciences do? The answer, from a social scientist: "It supplies knowledge that can be transmitted from person to person *qua* knowledge, here called 'intersubjectively transmissible knowledge,' or, briefly, 'transmissible knowledge.' " A bridge over the river *qua*. The *Individualized Learning Letter,* which is published in Huntington, New York, and goes to school administrators, has told of the working draft of a report whose recommendations "seek to free learning and teaching from the shackles of time, place and age, and to breach the real and imaginary walls that tend to make intermediate and secondary schools isolated islands for adolescents." The island that is not only an island but is isolated as well must be an extremely lonely place to be. But that aside, time, place, and age are not shackles. They are inescapable conditions of life, which would be unimaginable without them. Does it make no difference where you are? When? Whether you are five or fifteen or fifty? If education is in the hands of people who consider time, place, and age shackles, and who would like islands no longer to be isolated, I prefer that their knowledge not be transmissible and I would blow up the *qua* bridge to bring that about.

Bernice L. Neugarten, professor of human development in the Department of Behavioral Science at the University of Chicago, has written that "if the young-old do not form a strong age-group identification of their own, they may well become major agents of social change in moving toward the society in which age is irrelevant." If the young-old do form a strong age-group identification of their own, I would like to know what it is. ("We are the young-old. We are naughty but nice and sometimes have to be cruel to be kind.")

In January 1976 George Millar, principal of Tunn High School in Palo Alto, California, asked to be reassigned. "I have been here six years," Millar said, "and that is probably long enough for a person to be principal of one school. As a change agent, my utility as principal is probably done." A change agent who stays too long in one place may grow young-old before his time.

I expect to cling to the belief that age matters. In many aspects of our lives it is the controlling factor. One need only be young or old to appreciate this. There cannot be a society in which age is irrelevant.

There is much at stake in understanding this. The use of language that is at bottom nonsense leads, as might be expected, to the advocacy of nonsensical ideas and, by the law of averages alone, to the adoption of nonsensical ideas. At the least, the language and the ideas go hand in hand. Let us return, for another demonstration, to Nashville, home of country music and the Metro School Board. In the discussion of curriculum planning mentioned earlier, the Board announced that it intended "to facilitate the development process, with the ultimate goal of creating a flexible model for an interdisciplinary approach to teaching" that would "correlate subject areas whenever meaningful to make learning experiences a related integral whole."

A related integral whole was not the educational ambition of William C. Pratella, superintendent of schools in Mount Vernon, New York. He wanted—but let him tell it: "We will present all the subject areas—no established curriculum area will be neglected —and teach them as a unified whole to reveal their inherent interrelatedness."

This is as practicable an idea as making all the world kin. All the subject areas do not make a related integral whole, or a unified whole, except in a sense so loose as to be meaningless. Nor would it be a good idea if they did. Education is a voyage of discovery that may take you in many directions. That's half the fun of it. It is normal for young people to be tugged this way and that by new ideas* almost as soon as (phrasing courtesy of a high-school principal in Evansville, Indiana) they are mainstreamed into the classroom situation. Talk about making education a unified whole is sloganeering, churned out to create the impression that something complex and abstruse is taking place. It is done for self-preservation and self-promotion. The American Federation of Labor, when it was made up of craft unions only, practiced job-conscious unionism, meaning that its members were principally interested in protecting their jobs. So it is with educators who speak of revealing the inherent interrelatedness of established curriculum areas. By mystifying the public they protect their jobs

---

* This concept need not be expressed so starkly. From a discussion of imaginal education methods in a paper of the same name: "Since new data inconsistent with operating images can challenge those images, it is clear that learning is a perpetual dynamic of re-imaging the 'real.' " This won the package-of-the-year award in 1976.

and avoid the danger that they will be (educational language again) excessed.

Nor is this unusual. Few of us pump out the smog that educators do, but it is also true that few of us spend our lives risking all. I have not often gone to see the head of NBC News and said, "I have prospered enough. Excess me." If I did, I would be told in a kindly manner, "Excessing is not our way here, Newman. We fire people."

Avoiding being excessed may require obedience to behavioral objectives. I realize that I should pause here to define behavioral objectives, but it is not easy to do. The term appears to have as much reality as inherent interrelatedness does. I have a paper prepared by an education organization in Massachusetts that advocates setting behavioral objectives for students, teachers, and parents. It is full of such phrases as learning sequence, learning outcomes, the instructional process, a variety of media and methods, and effective diagnosis. It reaches its peak with the claim that teachers who adopt behavioral objectives will be able to "provide students with a pharmacy of learning alternatives matched to the objectives and tailored to the individual characteristics of each student."

Where pharmacies of learning alternatives exist—usually at the back of the drug store, past the lunch counter and the toilet articles—students are sent in with prescriptions to be filled. They are watched closely for side effects, and if there are any the prescription is changed. It is a perpetual dynamic.

Because many people who sent me material for a second book asked that the source not be revealed, I can only say that "A Note on Grading in Economics 596 and 597" came to me from Texas, where an institution of higher learning was offering these courses for credit toward a degree of Master of Arts in Manpower and Industrial Relations. As I read the Note, it struck me that those offering Economics 596 and 597 were setting behavioral objectives, perhaps without knowing it:

"Do you realize, Miss Compton, that you have established behavioral objectives?"

"Oh, doctor!"

The Note put it this way: "These tests . . . are . . . intended to provide us with information as to the effectiveness of our instructional system with respect to the achievement of our objectives. They will also serve as an index, for your use, of how well you have learned the treated material." That would be, in short, that through the tests the teachers and students would know what the students were learning. In short it never is.

Using the Socratic method, the Note establishes that the final examination will consist of a series of multiple-choice-type items, and then, pursuing itself relentlessly, asks, "What is a creditable performance on the final examination?" It answers: "While we are reluctant at this time to set a hard and fast benchmark on this matter, our present inclination is to set the standard at somewhere in the neighborhood of the 90% correct level." Somewhere in the neighborhood of is a soft and loose benchmark.

As an alternative (obtained at the pharmacy) to the final examination, students in Economics 596 and 597 were told that they could submit an instructional module. The module referred to here is not simply the period with a facilitator in a learning station mentioned earlier, but "involves the selection or construction of a technology which, when implemented, is likely to be effective in moving the student population in the class from the condition of not having what you want them to have to the condition of having what you want them to have." At West Point it might be the very module of a modern major-general.

I often wish that my correspondent in Texas had told me which university offered Economics 596 and 597. It would be rewarding to drop in and hear the exchange.

"Good morning, student population in the class."

"Good morning, type-teacher."

After this promising beginning, the teacher says that he is tired and cannot remember whether the class has already been moved to a condition of having what he wants it to have. There is a bedlam of cries from the student population, some haves, some have-nots. Others are silent, too much talk about the instructional module having given them throat modules. The teacher, a son of the Ould Sodule and mindful of the maxim, Spare the rodule and spoil the child, says he will codule them no longer, and all go back to work, including a set of twins who are as alike as two peas in a podule.

When I was in school and teachers were trying to move me from the before condition to the after, and without benefit of modules, which had yet to be discovered, behavior meant conduct, whether you were good or bad. "Edwin's behavior has been better this term," the report card might say, "but he still sometimes talks in the corridors and sulks when he is corrected."

Years later I heard an ingenious application of the word in a calypso sung by a performer known as Growler, which told of his being fended off by a woman: "She say, 'Growler, have some behavior.'" Growler's behavioral objective evidently was not achieved.

If only educators could be told to have some behavior, with the language of modules and the like put off limits to them. But they will not be denied. They are demon lovers. Princeton University's Center of International Studies has a World Order Studies Program in which, among other problems, behavioral problems are studied. Thus: "The behavioral aspects of world order studies include problems associated with the relation of the diverse national attitudes of the world's societies and cultures to the common denominator of values necessary to a viable world order, and the creation and development of linkages between domestic and international order."

It is not often that one finds viable and linkages* so close to each other, and with a common denominator of values hardly a step away, and it is only a matter of time before the linkages will have to be viable, and the common denominators and values as well. However, advanced thinkers are finding viability inadequate or—this has arrived—not adequate enough. When Senator Lloyd Bentsen of Texas dropped out of the contest for the Democratic

---

* Not to be confused with causal links.

nomination for President, the *New York Times* said that he had never been a genuinely viable candidate. Governor Hugh Carey has called for a New York City that is "strong, viable and revitalized." If it's viable, it doesn't have to be revitalized.

The leaflet on Princeton's World Order Studies Program, a credit to the Ivy League, contains frames of reference, frameworks of action, normative aspects, the global community, normative implications, allocative institutions, political dimensions, resource utilization, and critical concepts, all being examined for the welfare of humankind.

Scene in the World Order Studies Program supply room:

"I need a critical concept, Jenkins."

"No trouble, sir. They're right here. They arrived this morning and we put them on the shelves at once. Any particular kind?"

"Yes, it should be a concept that is critical to the political dimensions of the problem."

"Would you like it sent?"

"Please. I also need a normative aspect, Jenkins."

"Sorry, sir, we're out of them. The demand has been heavy. I can give you a normative implication. There are a few of them left."

"Why weren't more aspects ordered?"

"I don't know, sir. That's a matter of resource utilization, and I'm only a clerk, sir. I have no allocative function. I can tell you that the implications come in a larger carton."

"All right, if that's all you have. Let me have one."

"What size, sir?"

"What do you mean, what size?"

"Broad or narrow, sir. Broad implications or narrow?"

"Broad, of course. Do you ever get orders for the other kind?"

"I'd rather not say, sir."

The appeal of this language lies in its slipperiness. It sounds as though it means something, especially to those who do not look at it closely. It serves as a fence that keeps others outside and respectful, or leads them to ignore what is going on because it is too much trouble to find out. For those inside, either effect is useful.

Language is used in this way in art, especially in painting. A press release issued by the Artemisia Gallery in Chicago was passed along to me. It said:

"Susan Michod's paintings have to do with multiplicity, ambiguity, and the layering of meanings. The basic drawing of the forms implies and denies a perspectival structure. This duality, also operating in the systematic use of color, value and pattern, pits three-dimensionality and flatness against each other. The slight wrinkling of the surface and fabric-like feel add elements of realistic illusionism to the formalist game-play. All of these elements are subservient to each other and the resulting complexity produces a shifting non-relational surface.

"The lack of dominance and the resulting non-hierarchical structure is a visual metaphor for a philosophical attitude about complexity, existentialism, feminism, and the absence of absolutes in our culture."

It is sad to see three-dimensionality and flatness pitted against each other. Both are known to be merciless and have reputations for stopping at nothing, and the presence of multiplicity, ambiguity, and the layering of meanings can only spur them on. But I suppose that that is the name of the formalist game-play.

The Artemisia press release is a child's primer compared with an article, "Formative Hermeneutics in the Arting Processes of an Other: The Philetics of Art Education," in the magazine *Art Education*. Its author was Kenneth R. Beittel, professor of art education at Pennsylvania State University. Here are some samples:

"The divided voice of the artist is taken up for and with him, the path unseen by the artist is allowed to announce itself, the past of the artist more strangely and as 'othered' enters his present and future, and his meeting with 'the other' is nonallergically extended and present 'face to face.' "

Now take a deep breath and go on.

"In terms of arting, where the reference condition is not fixed or even known conceptually but rather something coming to being, what can we hope through our formative hermeneutic movement? To make the 'otherness' of the arting process more other, more 'objective' in a newer sense and less 'subjective' in the older sense, so that the arting process itself speaks more purely?"

A further observation by Professor Beittel: "This is the very effect, then, that would strengthen the formative hermeneutic impact within the ongoing arting process. Here is no intervention, but an advent, in which the witness-as-sharer turns to co-agent. It is a shared adventure. . . . Thus, artist, witness and aborning work stand in relation: artist-witness, artist-work, and witness-work. A trinitarian co-agency, co-sharing, co-creating, transcending but not usurping autonomous otherness, but as in-relation, as in-between, is what is involved. While I believe this makes interpretation even harder, that is not a restriction to be imposed where the truth of being is the first concern. And, since anyone who has experienced essential being feels called upon to speak, the problem becomes that of how to speak."

The problem is, indeed, how to speak.

An invaluable piece of information appeared in capital letters, EXCESSIVE ANGER IN THE HOME IS DESTRUCTIVE TO SELF-IMAGE DEVELOPMENT, in a press release put out by Harper & Row for a book called WHAT EVERY CHILD NEEDS, by Lillian and Richard Peairs. I think of myself as EDWIN NEWMAN, and where possible in bold face as well as capitals, so my attention was caught at once. What every child needed, it turned out, was a positive creative image, a positive verbal image, a positive intellectual image, a positive ability image, a positive behavior image,* a positive physical image, and a positive social image. The only kind the child was thought not to need, evidently, was a positive image image, a serious flaw in the argument, for the absence of a positive image image may lead to what psychiatrists call identity diffusion, a state characterized by a lack of concept of self and a lack of concept of others,† which is as many concepts of the kind as it is possible to get along without.

It is sad to meet someone who lacks a positive image image.

---

* Growler did not have this.
† In dealing with this, formative hermeneutics may help.

I have heard more than one cast-down adult say, on being asked why he went about drooping and woebegone, that it was because he did not have a positive image of his self-image. "My self-image is fine," they would say. "I'm proud of myself. But I doubt that my self-image is justified."

In February 1976, on "Meet the Press," Helen Thomas of United Press International mentioned President Ford's "image portrayal problem." Ford had a positive creative-verbal-intellectual-ability-behavior-physical-social self-image. The problem Ms. Thomas referred to was that, at the time, some others doubted that his self-image was justified.

In June 1976 Leslie H. Gelb of the *New York Times* wrote that Henry Kissinger was suffering from bad imagery. Criticizing a Secretary of State for lacking the poetic touch seemed to be going a little far, but Gelb explained himself. Conservatives, he said, saw Kissinger as Rasputin, anti-Semites saw him as Shylock, and liberals saw him as George III. Rasputin, Shylock, and George would make a formidable and versatile triumvirate, especially if one accepts the recent opinion of historians that George was not insane but only sick and in need of help, but none of them fits Kissinger's self-image, at any rate as publicly revealed.

Because the absence of self-images can be crippling, the task of developing self-acceptable self-images is welcomed by many institutions. The United States Navy's Finance Center, in Cleveland, offers Participative Management Training, a task-oriented training experience directed toward improvement of interpersonal skills. It is craftily devised to bring optimal (best is not enough) results by making attendance completely (not partly) voluntary.

A quick overview of the course, from an article in the *Journal of Navy Civilian Manpower Management:*

"Our adaptation includes the use of several structured consensus tasks, exposure to the Blake and Mouton Managerial Grid, and experience with the Johari Window. We use several instruments to assist participants in appraising their leadership styles and in planning for change. We intersperse through the institute lecturettes on McGregor's Theory X and Theory Y, Maslow's hierarchy of needs, and Herzberg's motivator and hygiene factors. The entire institute is task-oriented."

The paragraph insistently brings to mind the triumphs of other naval task-oriented forces:

Damn the motivator factors! Optimal speed ahead!

Don't give up the lecturettes!

The Animal and Health Inspection Service of the Agriculture Department offers women employees seminars in assertive awareness. The seminars consist of lectures (no lecturettes that insultingly suggest that those listening have a short attention span), discussions, and Danish thumb wrestling. According to R. M. Gurley, the service's training officer, the seminars tone down women on the "super-aggressive, super-hostile side" and help the shy and reticent to deal with their male supervisors. In Danish thumb wrestling, hands are locked in such a way that only the thumbs are free to do battle. Each tries to push the other down. The cost of the seminars to the middle of 1976 was $44,000. The Danes say that thumb wrestling has nothing to do with them.

Institutions have images of themselves, also. "The goal of the U.C.C. is the development of well-rounded persons. It encourages self-directed activity, while giving maximum opportunity for self-realization and for growth in individual self-competency and group effectiveness."*

This last comes, advocates of hemispheric solidarity will be gratified to learn, from Canada. The U.C.C. is the University Community Centre of the University of Western Ontario, London, Canada. Functioning, as it points out, within the framework of the community concept, the U.C.C. has a bookstore which "considers its role to be to create the broadest possible interface of the world of information packages and the whole university community, and to serve as a retail outlet on campus to fulfill other service requirements." This means that the bookstore sells

---

* Self-directed activity sounds as though it would direct itself, which would be humiliating for a well-rounded, self-realized, self-competent, group-effective person.

books. Though a country with a relatively small population, Canada can interface with the best of them.

All right, the second best of them, because Canada cannot interface with Sanford M. Lewis, M.D., of East Orange, New Jersey, who wrote to the *New York Times,* "I too am concerned with the evolution of viable constructs by which complex problems at the medical-legal interface can be effectively resolved for social usefulness." Even against Canada, practiced in ice hockey though it is, Dr. Lewis wins the interface-off.

I have gone to the medical-legal interface only on journalistic assignment, and with hazardous duty pay, but I did go one day on my own time to an interfaith interface. As luck would have it, my ecumenical mood was curdled by the realization that the meeting was troubled by multivariate problems, among them the fact that some of those attending were, like the Japanese, interested only in saving interface, while others were there only in search of interaction that might lead to interpersonal relations, such as going elsewhere and dancing intercheek. I decided to interface up to the fact that I would probably never again attend such a meeting, for I knew that many of the interpersonal relations begun there would end unhappily, possibly even in a category to which a sociologist at the University of Southern California consigned murder and assault—escalated interpersonal altercations. But that was a long way off. I was reminded of the summarizative description of the aims of a research project on romantic love financed by the National Science Foundation:

"The primary aim of this research project is to examine the role of psychological dependency as an antecedent to interpersonal attraction, particularly, though not exclusively, in heterosexual relationships in which the individuals involved label their attraction 'romantic love.' A related, but subsidiary, aim is to assess the potential of the dependency construct to provide the core of a theoretical framework whose predictive domain would encompass not only the milder forms of attraction, such as 'liking' and 'disliking,' but also the stronger forms, such as 'love' and 'hate,' in both like- and opposite-sex relationships. An examination of the relationships between hypothesized dependency variables will be made, as well as an examination of the effect which environmental conditions conducive and nonconducive to fantasy may have upon these variables. Too, the investigation of situational factors which may determine labeling of positive affect in dyadic relationships will be undertaken. Research will involve both laboratory and field investigation."

A bargain at $133,400, though not likely to enrich the language:

"It's no use fighting it, baby. You and I have an interpersonal attraction in an opposite-sex relationship going."

"Take it easy, big boy. You don't understand. In the first place, we're crosscultural. In the second place, the moon is an environmental condition conducive to fantasy. And there are situational factors that may determine positive affect. We are, to put it plainly, the only ones here."

"You're wrong, baby. This is a dyadic relationship if I ever saw one. It's the real thing."

Suddenly she yields. The positive affect is too strong. Her resistance to a dependency construct self-destructs. He works his will on her. They interface.

Interfacing is not always so intense and interpersonal. The Energy Research and Development Administration has published, in the *Federal Register,* a Consumer Representation Plan that "focuses on two functions: Information Input and Information Output." ERDA* announced that it planned to accelerate communication, glean feedback, finalize option papers, make a concentrated and time-constrained effort, and use new public outreach interlocking mechanisms to broaden and sharpen the interface process. The public outreach interlocking mechanisms sound as

---

* The initials were chosen to make up an acronym standing for Erda, the earth goddess, who when not otherwise occupied sings in *Das Rheingold* and *Siegfried* in Wagner's *Ring.* Nobody ever accused Wagner of accelerating communication or making a time-constrained effort.

though they will cancel each other, but that can happen when government agencies go at things in a rush. Time constraint makes waste.

If all government agencies are intent on interfacing, however, there is reason to doubt that there will be enough concerned citizens to go around. Citizens we have in plenty; concerned citizens are so scarce that they have to be shared almost constantly among government departments, wearing a worried look when providing input and evincing relief and enlightenment when receiving output. Some of the citizens were exhausted by overuse and tumbled into the outreach interlocking mechanisms, which had to be interrupted in their broadening and sharpening and brought grinding to a halt. It does appear that a CCC (Concerned Citizens Corps) is needed. However, the demand for a CCC may be reduced by the creation, under a law passed in 1974, of the Office of Federal Procurement Policy. The OFPP's administrator, Hugh E. Witt, has said, "We are the interface* between the executive branch and industry." Witt may be able to procure concerned citizens and distribute them in areas of greatest need.

Outreaching and interfacing in their beginning stages may be seen in a letter written by the environmental review officer of a city in the Middle West. He was asking those with the same job in other cities for help:

"Dear Sir:

"Recently this department became aware of the crucial need to collect sufficient technical information and thereby to implement the methodology of environmental analysis in urban planning. Toward this formidable endeavor, we have researched available information and those organizations displaying excellence in this venue. We therefore wish to present a respectful request for repre-

---

* I was present at a meeting in June 1976 at which a participant said that one of the problems facing us was the lack of a structured interface. I mention this to show that I write about these matters from experience and bear the scars of combat.

sentative examples of environmental and developmental analysis which you have available.

"Our progress to this point in utilizing fundamental environmental requisites is represented by the creation of a manual, but soon to be computerized, environmental data base. Further, we are incorporating existing staff expertise and planning process derived from conventional physical and computer planning capabilities. But, without some superior paradigms which depict attainments made on the 'cutting edge' of technical innovation, we will experience an obvious delay in the 'tool up' phase prior to the urgently needed application.

"If you could perhaps forward several such environmental studies and/or other development feasibility research, or provide referral as to the means and cost of procurement, we would be most appreciative. Any similar assistance which we might provide from our subsequent efforts would certainly be yours promptly upon request. . . .

"Sincerely."

There are briefer ways of putting it—"Brother, can you spare a superior paradigm?"

I cannot believe that anybody well stocked with paradigms could resist the heartfelt yearning evident in the letter. It is, however, as well that only urban planning paradigms were needed because certain other kinds are not readily obtainable. I base this comment on an essay in a book titled *Against the World, For the World,* which looks at the future of American religion. In it the language of the social sciences takes possession of religion, a conversion in keeping with the times.

George Lindbeck, of the Yale Divinity School, who wrote the essay, believes that we are living through a paradigm shift, and that the old paradigms seem increasingly inadequate and the new ones implausible. Lindbeck acknowledges that his conclusion depends "on the adequacy of a paradigm-shift analysis of theological crises," but he does not doubt that a revolution in theological paradigms is going on. Paradigm-shift analysis is not my field—I have no training in it; but paradigms, one gathers with Lindbeck's guidance, do not last forever. The time comes when one says, " 'Twere paradigm enow."*

Christopher Mwoleka is the Roman Catholic Bishop of Rulenge, in Tanzania, and lives in the village of Nyabihinga. Bishop Mwoleka might be thought to be burning with a desire to save souls. Not so. He told a reporter that he wants the villages to be "oriented to God." As social science language goes, that is only a beginning, but Nyabihinga, Tanzania, gets sketchy service from the social sciences. Bishop Mwoleka could hardly expect to equal this statement by Paul Lehmann in *The Transfiguration of Politics: The Presence and Power of Jesus of Nazareth in and over Human Affairs,* published in 1975 by Harper & Row:

"Piety and politics belong intrinsically and inseparably together. Piety is the compound of reverence and thankfulness that forms and transforms the reciprocity between creaturehood and creativity, in privacy and in society, into the possibility and the power of fulfilling human freedom and joy. Politics is the compound of justice, ordination, and order that shapes, sustains, and gives structure to a social matrix for the human practice of privacy and for the practice of humanness in community. In such a matrix, justice is the reciprocity of differences in creaturehood and creativity, experienced as enrichment rather than as a threat; ordination is the insistent priority and pressure of purpose over power in the practice of the reciprocity between creaturehood and creativity; and order is the possibility and the power of so living in one time and place as not to destroy the possibility of other times and places. So piety apart from politics loses its integrity and converts into apostasy; whereas politics without piety subverts both its divine ordination and its ordering of humanness, perverts justice, and converts into idolatry.

"To read and understand the Bible politically and to under-

---

* The pronunciation, I am sorry to say, is paradim, which eliminates "One kiss, one fond caress, They lead the way to happiness, They take me to paradigm." However, it does make possible paradiminuendo, which is a model no longer much followed.

stand and practice politics biblically is to discern in, with, and under the concrete course of human events the presence and power of God at work, giving human shape to human life. The human meaning of politics is to the biblical meaning of politics as the Fall is to the creaturehood and destiny of humanity in a world that has been created and redeemed."

The point, I believe, is that the Biable is viable.

It is possible that neither the man who wants his environmental data base brought up to date nor any of the three theologians just quoted has ever met a payroll, an experience thought in some circles to produce individuals who are matter-of-fact, hard-bitten, and laconic. (The hard biters of the hard-bitten have never been identified.) Nonetheless, people who do meet payrolls speak contemporary American. In a speech to the American Life Insurance Association Convention in San Francisco, in December 1974, Allan D. Schuster, vice president and general manager, Citicorp Realty Consultants, Inc., of New York City, posed this question: "Are we watching a recurring phenomenon or is real estate on the road toward stability shaped by forces of positive change at war with the old ways?" Having cornered himself, Schuster replied that out of the crisis was coming an emerging professionalism. He epitomized this by dropping into his speech ongoing, conceptual, expertise, viability, highly-leveraged, contained multi-purpose communities, societal attitudes, benchmarks, over-leveraged, and macro market research. Research, Schuster let it be known, was indispensable. Holy macro.

Contemporary American is also spoken by trade unionists. Ben Fisher, special assistant to the president of the United Steelworkers of America, was quoted in *New Times* magazine on the question of discrimination against blacks in the steel industry: "It is just not accurate to believe that blacks were confined somehow to the lowest paying jobs; rather, there was some tendency for blacks to be congregated in certain units which had a variety of characteristics including, in some instances, a somewhat lower average pay than some units where there might be a heavy concentration of white employees." Meaning, apparently, that blacks who received lower pay than whites did not have lower paying jobs. Bring back the young-old.

An employment agency in New York, the Craig Computer Centre Agency, sent the personnel managers of companies it dealt with a letter that began with these words: "The purpose of this letter is to historize the philosophical infrastructure Craig Computer Centre abides, regarding applicant referrals." The agency wanted to tell its customers what its policy was. Instead, it historized the philosophical infrastructure Craig Computer Centre abides. I cherish the hope that anybody who historizes philosophical infrastructures will abide not with me, but that they will abide and prosper is certain. They are everywhere. Here is an infrastructure from the August 1975 issue of the *Designer*, published by the American Society of Interior Designers:

"There is a wide gap between multi-disciplinary teams and inter-disciplinary teams. Multi-disciplinary applies when various disciplines provide their views with minimal cooperative interaction. Interdisciplinarity requires coordination among disciplines and synthesis of material through a higher-level organizing concept. . . .

"A good test of interdisciplinarity is whether a team can integrate imaginative ideas originating from different disciplinary perspectives so that the work product reflects an expanded lens of perception of reality."

These views were contributed to the *Designer* by Sherry R. Arnstein, of the Academy for Contemporary Problems. Ms. Arnstein is in the right academy.

Scene in the disciplinary barracks:

"Bad news, Graustark. You're going down to the multis."

"Gee, Sergeant, I thought I was doing so well."

"You were for a while, Graustark. But the inters are too fast for you. Still, look at it this way. Multidisciplinarity is better than unidisciplinarity."

"Unidisciplinarity?"

"Solitary."

"What am I doing wrong, Sergeant? Is it my work product?"

"It's more basic, Graustark. It's your lens of perception of reality. It won't expand."

More modest than the interdisciplinary or multidisciplinary team is the transbinary, which brings together two disciplines (stern and lax), and which has a lens barely open at all. Transbinary is well established in Britain, where transbinary collaboration between universities is encouraged, but it is only at the beginning of its career in the United States. Remember, you heard it here first.

# A Fatal Slaying
## of the Very Worst Kind

I t is typical of American English that enough is almost never enough. Is there a famine? No, there are famine conditions. Are there kinds of molecules, or ice cream, or postcards, or whatever they may be? No, there are different kinds. Is it the hottest Easter Sunday we've ever had? It is the hottest Easter Sunday we've ever had, regardless of date. When House Speaker Carl Albert announced that he would retire at the end of 1976, was Thomas O'Neill of Massachusetts the heir apparent? Not at all. According to United Press International, he was the apparent heir apparent. Does Jimmy Carter's pollster, Patrick Caddell, give his client, Saudi Arabia, information in confidence? He would rather speak of "the confidentiality of my client situation." Is there an urban crisis? No, said Morris Udall on April 17, 1976, there is an urban crisis situation. Is Italy's economy deteriorating? No, said Edwin Newman of NBC News in a broadcast in May 1976, Italy is in a deteriorating economic situation.

We no longer have rules and prospects and news but ground rules, future prospects, and newsworthy happenings. Airlines tell us to read the instructions in the seat pocket in front of us not for our safety but for our personal safety. Companies do not grow; they enjoy positive growth. The Encinitas Union School District in California announces that it will provide equal employment opportunity not merely through affirmative action but through positive affirmative action. Do new cameras obviate special lighting? They obviate the need for special lighting. Is the horse Rogue's Gambit, subject of a story in the *Washington Post,* one of a kind? No, it is uniquely one of a kind. Does Nelson Rockefeller complain of a misrepresentation by Ronald Reagan? No, he complains of a factual misrepresentation, which cancels itself. Was a woman raped? No, she had a rape experience. Shall we face reality? We can do better. We can face reality as it is. Pillows renovated, a shop proclaims, like new. No trespassing, signs say, without permission.

All this is redundancy, to which Americans have become addicted. We ought to have signs posted that say, "No redundancy without permission." Still, if you have a sunny disposition, there is always comfort to be found somewhere, and I would rather be redundant in the American sense than in the British.

In Britain someone who loses his job is not thereby rendered unemployed or out of work. He is made redundant. A company will not say that it is going to lay people off. It warns that there will be redundancies. The BBC and the newspapers headline Redundancies at Coventry or Cowley or wherever it may be; the British comedian Spike Milligan fifteen years ago invented a character whose occupation was retired redundant.

In the great days of American western movies, the sheriff would often choose some hapless fellow who did not want to become involved, pin a star on him, and say, "I'm namin' yew my deppity." In somewhat the same way the British look at workers and name them redundant, or in the North of England, redoondant. The difference is that the redundants would rather be deputized, and the deppities would rather be redundant.

Given the addiction to jargon among statisticians and among

social scientists generally, it is surprising* that redundant, in the sense of out of work, has not caught on in the United States. The British borrow from us indiscriminately and no questions asked. They—quick learners—are having major confrontations, consulting in depth, satisfying targets, giving the score situation instead of the score, flaunting instead of flouting, making an effort to try, subjecting clothes not to washing but to water process treatment, describing the way people talk as their conversation culture, and—in prestige projects—describing swimming pools and playing fields as leisure complexes. They are also calling for action on a broad front, particularly in areas of cultural disadvantage; making controversial recommendations and advocating controversial teaching methods; holding major official inquiries; lavishing each other with gifts; discussing the country's intervention capability; issuing consultative documents; looking on with approval as disadvantaged children verbalize to their peers; transmuting guest stars into special guest stars; and setting preconditions, which somehow surpass conditions and, when they number more than one, become packages. The BBC has even broadcast a song called, "Life Is the Name of the Game."

In return we should be borrowing from the British, if only on a small scale. It seems the least we could do. However, redundant in the sense of unemployed will never catch on with us. Redundancy in language has preempted the field. Because it has, much American speech and writing is boring, wastes time and effort, and makes reading and conversation a chore. We slog through the laborious and repetitious, and tarry when we should be moving on. Redundancy's cause is triumphant.† A Viking scientist, asked whether the loss of an instrument would mean that the soil-collecting scoop would not function, replied: "No. We have redundancy in that area." By that standard, no car should be without a redundant tire.

Irving S. Shapiro, chairman of the board and chief executive officer of Du Pont, has denied that the company interfered in the

---

* And unexpected. Read on.

† Successfully triumphant. Read on.

editing of two newspapers Du Pont owns in Wilmington, Delaware. "Emphatically not true," he said. Then, the emphatically being not emphatic enough, Shapiro added, "And there are no solid facts which would support a contrary inference."

I once came upon a solid fact that was supporting a contrary inference, and, possibly because the pedestal was Corinthian and the capital Ionic, it was an ill-assorted solid fact and was cracking under the strain. Shapiro did not mention the facts that were once so popular with politicians and editorial writers, the true facts, no doubt because they have been displaced—not in Britain, where the playwright William Douglas-Home has implored the Conservative Party to keep plugging, day in and day out, the true facts about taxation, but in the United States. A press release for Quinn Martin Productions about a television film based on events in Mississippi in the summer of 1964 noted that "the facts hew to actuality." Facts that hew to actuality open up—here I am indebted to Charles Prince of Wales and his splendid English education—new and previously undiscovered vistas. Those who ignore facts that hew to actuality do so at their own risk. In a barbarous world they may suffer the fate that the Prince cheerfully noted befell one of his ancestors. Said ancestor subsequently lost his head at a later date.

I am, of course, discussing what Secretary of State Kissinger called a hypothetical situation that does not now exist. It is only when a hypothetical situation does exist that it warrants our concern. If it is pressing and appears to threaten our security, we may want to get, perhaps from Pentagon spokesman Joseph Laitin, a preliminary final count on which of our allies will stand with us. Preliminary final will have to do because—here again the felicitous phrase was Kissinger's—it will be too early to draw a final conclusion. Those who want to draw conclusions will have to use the nonfinal variety.

When I mention a final conclusion I am speaking in terms of terms. Moderator Bill Monroe on "Meet the Press," November 30, 1974: "I think our time is up in terms of having time for another question." Etcyl H. Blair, director of health and environmental research for Dow Chemical USA: ". . . a series of question-able restrictions have had unfavorable impacts on American workers, in terms of lost job opportunities; on consumers, in terms of higher costs and fewer choices; and on scientists, in terms of lost incentive and lost confidence."

In terms of being necessary, in terms of isn't. Reviewing the PBS series on health, "Feeling Good," in the *New York Times,* John O'Connor remarked that it was "attempting to reach a broader audience in terms of national coverage." He could have said broader national audience and let it go at that. In the same review O'Connor wrote that "Feeling Good" resembles a variant of "The Electric Company," which must be subtly different from resembling "The Electric Company" itself, and that he thought it had been designed for a slightly, but not much, older audience.

Of "Feeling Good" he said in conclusion, "No one may be thoroughly offended, but no one is likely to be adequately satisfied, either." A lack of adequate satisfaction is frustrating, but then, slightly but not much older audiences are known to be slightly if not much harder to please. They seldomly* go in for what O'Connor called, in reviewing the CBS situation comedy "One Day at a Time," loud shouting.†

When a forty-five-year-old man from Sanford, Maine, claimed to be the son of Anne and Charles Lindbergh, David Wilentz, the New Jersey prosecutor in the Lindbergh baby kidnaping case, was asked for his reaction. Said Wilentz: "Preposterous and" (there is always an and) "beyond the realm of possibility." Maybe loud shouting, preliminary final, hypothetical situations that do not exist, and preposterous and beyond the realm of possibility are only to be expected. The United States is the most wasteful

---

* Hank Stram, former coach of the Kansas City Chiefs, became a football broadcaster and wondered, during the 1976 Super Bowl, why Dallas threw the ball very seldomly. He seemed unaware that its passes had oftenly been intercepted.

† Loud shouting may be done individually or, as at college athletic contests, in mass unison. The *New York Times* sometimes alternates it with loud yelling.

country in the world, and our use of words is extravagant. The waste has two causes. One is the feeling not seldomly encountered that an idea is more effective if it is repeated and reinforced. This is why Jimmy Carter says that he had a deeply profound religious experience. At any rate, I want to believe that that is why. I would hate to learn that he thought that deep and profound are different. It is certainly why Harper & Row announced early in 1976 that the paperback rights to one of its books had been sold for a "substantial six-figure sum." Even with inflation there is no sizable school of thought that holds six-figure sums to be paltry. I agree that this depends on where you are—life in some urban cities is more expensive than in others, as many a future bride-to-be learns to her sorrow after she is married—and whether you are touched by the revolution of rising expectations. In the late 1940s the former attorney general of California, Robert Kenny, represented a client before a congressional committee in Washington. Kenny's client was distressed about something that had been said about him and had brought a suit for damages. "How much are you suing for, Mr. Kenny?" a reporter asked. Kenny seemed surprised by the question. "The usual million," he said.

The second cause of waste is a failure to understand what words mean. The *New York Times* could not run a headline about an unexpected surprise from Japan if it knew what surprise meant. If it understood what triumph meant, it could not, in reporting an interview with Representative Les Aspin of Wisconsin, describe a spending ceiling on a defense authorization bill as "perhaps his most successful triumph." Aspin probably kept his less successful triumphs to himself, or the *Times* would have trumpeted them as triumphant Pyrrhic victories. *Harper's* magazine, speculating on a replacement for Henry Kissinger as Secretary of State, identified a former diplomat who had successfully convinced much of the foreign affairs community that he was a profound thinker. In view of the new requirement for deep profundity, this may not be enough.

Senator Charles Percy of Illinois, when he had some hope of getting the Republican presidential nomination in 1976, announced that he could be found in the "centrist mainstream" of American politics. It did not help Percy, but, generally speaking, it is a good place for a politician to be. An officer of the Ford election committee recognized this during the Republican primaries. "Ford has got to be pictured in the mainstream," he said, "and Reagan off on the right bank, so to speak." The officer understood that away from the bulrushes and down the centrist mainstream float Presidents and bills that have a good chance of being, in the words of the *New York Times,* successfully passed or, failing that, successfully enacted. Bills from the extremist mainstream do not automatically come under—again in the words of the *New York Times*—a total ban. They may even—*New York Times*—successfully withstand attacks, in spite of earlier impressions that they would unsuccessfully withstand them. Their sponsors may make an effort to try (Senator Birch Bayh) to successfully capture supporters (United Press International) where none had been thought to exist. ("Aha! In my power! Successfully captured at last!") But sooner or later the bill from the right bank or the left will be seen to be coming from one who is only an occasional frequenter (*Gourmet magazine*) of the centrist mainstream, and the bill will be (*New York Times*) successfully stifled.

*Time* magazine has noted that the National Football League successfully avoided any direct brush with gambling interests from 1963 to 1974, evidently for the benefit of those who thought that the League had unsuccessfully avoided them. *Time* speaks of arguments that were not successfully refuted and of fugitives who successfully eluded their pursuers, and says that the Broadway musical *Candide* was played on an open stage surrounded on all sides by the audience. Encircled on a couple of sides though I was by other assignments, I continued reading *Time* and was rewarded by the news that Rhodesia found itself not merely surrounded by hostile African governments but completely surrounded by them.

I. F. Stone, in the *New York Review of Books,* tells us that it was John Wilkes who established the right of the press to cover parliamentary proceedings when, as Sheriff of London, he successfully prevented the arrest of a printer the House of Commons had charged with publishing its debates. An ounce of successful prevention is worth a pound of successful cure, which explains why Ronald R. Fieve, M.D., chief of psychiatric research at the Lithium Clinic and Metabolic Unit in New York City, hopes to prevent successful suicides among his patients; why another doctor sympathizes with a patient suffering from subjective pain and another reports on tonsils that could not be entirely removed in toto; why countries—Rhodesia is an example—are said to declare unilateral independence, as though there were any other kind; why United Press International speaks of people being rescued safely; why TWA, delivering an unaccompanied child to its parent, guardian, or some other designated person, calls it a positive handoff; why reporters who do what used to be known as reporting are called investigative reporters, and biographers who do what biographers should do are said to write investigative biographies; and why David Sencer, director of the National Center for Disease Control, does not say that an epidemic is passing but that "there is a downslope on the curve of occurrence." Does a downward trend wipe out the previous day's sharp gains by the dollar? It does not. It—United Press International—wipes them out completely.

UPI is often on top of the news:

"Miami (UPI)—A Puerto Rican who said he attempted unsuccessfully to shoot President Ford on Saturday has been charged with threatening the life of the President."

UPI must have been relieved to hear that the attempt was unsuccessful. Otherwise somebody in the Miami bureau might have become redundant.

Dr. John Lundgren, looking after Richard Nixon, said in January 1975, "He still tires and fatigues very easily." When you tire and fatigue, you are really worn out. Lieutenant General James F. Hollingsworth, United States commander in South Korea, said that if the North Koreans attack, "Our firepower will have a tremendous impact on their ground troops, breaking their will in addition to killing them." This dual purpose explains why the United States must have sophisticated weapons.

Hollingsworth's language may have been influenced by his colleague, or as some now have it, his fellow colleague, Major General Henry E. "Gunfighter" Emerson. When President Ford stopped off to visit the Second Division in Korea on his way to the Soviet Union in November 1974, Emerson prepared his men for the President's arrival with these words:

"He's not just our Commander-in-Chief. He's Commander-in-Chief of all the American troops. He's Commander-in-Chief of the whole free world, and he's going to talk to the Russian Communists. He's a hell of a man. He's an All-American football player, and I guess that tells you what kind of a guy he is. He's putting our country back together and he's putting the world back together."

If the language seems more suitable to an inspiring talk by a gutsy coach in a somber locker room at half-time, it should be borne in mind that General Emerson was not getting his men merely ready. In Pentagon parlançe, he was getting them operationally ready. Nor were they to join in the country's defense. They were to take their place in the country's defense posture, a responsibility far weightier and more compelling, which is why the Pentagon issues an annual defense posture statement. During the 1976 contest for the Republican presidential nomination, one of the issues between Ford and Reagan was whether the United States military posture was declining. If decline goes far enough, a low profile results.

Jimmy Carter also spoke of the country's military posture. He wanted it reviewed. In addition, he said that the Warsaw Pact forces were "postured for an all-out conflict of short duration and great intensity." In an interview on foreign affairs Carter had this country "in the posture quite often of having to face an accomplished fact of our adjustment of our interests," and endorsed a "rough equivalency" with the Russians as "a very good posture to maintain." Carter must have wanted to leave Plains, Georgia, for Washington and greener postures.

For a man whose political fortunes rested on his not being

associated in the public mind with Washington, Carter took risks. In one speech on foreign affairs he mentioned not only a military and a recent posture but ever increasing unity and understanding, a significant world impact, larger global roles, a new international order, democratic values, political and economic concerns, frequent consultations on many levels, our entire foreign policy apparatus, continuing contacts at all levels, closer and more creative relations, increased coordination among the industrialized democracies, multilateral trade negotiations, basic monetary adjustments, interactions among national economies, a creative partnership, basic global standards of human rights, our own basic ideals, the democratic process, the democratic concert of nations, the strategic umbrella, a pressing need, genuine North-South consultations, sharper confrontations, a more stable and just world order, a major effort, and global economic development. Not exactly a new broom.

Not all postures are military. Henry Kissinger was sometimes said to need a more credible posture in Latin America. This lies somewhere between bending over backward and being standoffish. I was round-shouldered as a boy, which is the opposite of bending over backward, and was often scolded about it. "Straighten up, Edwin," my mother used to say. Questions about my credibility arose in other connections.*

In Washington one day, after President Ford vetoed a bill to which he had given active, rather than inactive or passive, consideration, the Senate overrode the veto by seventy-two to one. The *San Francisco Chronicle* felt obliged to note that seventy-two to one was "well over the two-thirds majority needed." This comes

---

* Discussion of somebody's credibility usually means that credibility is something he does not have. Credibility results from a proportion between what you say you will do and what your interests make it reasonable for you to do. It may also arise from being erratic and unpredictable, in which case others will be reluctant to find out whether you mean what you say. The credibility of nuclear deterrents cannot be tested without risking annihilation. There is an old line that covers the situation: Take my word for it.

under the head of interpretive reporting. The veto was of a Railroad Retirement bill that reflected many hopes and aspirations. These now make up one word in Washington—hopesandaspirations—and so technically do not constitute a redundancy. Hopesandaspirations will soon be joined by necessaryandessential, unnecessaryandsuperfluous, fairandequitable, loudandvociferous, goalsandobjectives, helpandassistance, promptandspeedy, procrastinationanddelay, adviceandcounsel, interestandconcern, and reputationfortruthandveracity, which comes from the legal world, where it appears to be thought that a witness can have a well-deserved reputation for telling the truth without having veracity.

Justandlasting and ournation'scapital may appear to belong in the list, but they are not redundancies. They are clichés and they drain words of their meaning. The redundancy also weakens words by implying that they cannot stand alone—advice *and* counsel. In addition, it clutters the language. It impedes the communication that Americans insist they so dearly want by making it necessaryandessential to hack away what is not necessaryandessential to get to the point. I will settle for either goals or objectives and for either equitable or fair, and consider myself well served.

Precision in language can be delightful and devastating. I know this from experience. As a glamorous and commanding figure on the screen, and even more winning and vivacious in person, I am sometimes asked why I do not smile more often while performing. The answer has to do with a program in 1961, on which I appeared with Hugh Gaitskell, then leader of the British Labour Party, and Walter Judd, then a Republican Representative from Minnesota.

My performance was so striking that the mail poured in, in the form of a letter from a clergyman in Connersville, Indiana, who accused me of, without also charging me with, smirking at Representative Judd. The NBC News executive who answered the letter replied that this surely could not have taken place since a smirk was an expression revealing inner malice and that was not part of my disposition. The clergyman replied that in his view and according to a dictionary that lay to hand, a smirk was a smug, silly, self-satisfied smile and that was part of my disposition. We dropped the correspondence.

Since the Judd incident, I have tried to keep a dead pan, and some might say that I have one presently. *Harper's* magazine probably would, if it thought about the matter, because *Harper's* has an unfortunate way of saying that one of its contributors is presently writing a book, or presently completing a novel. Presently is unnecessary in these phrases as well as ill-advised because the primary meaning of presently is soon. Dictionaries ought to insist on that. Giving way and allowing it to mean now—over which, for some people, it has the great advantage of being two syllables longer—creates confusion. It creates almost as much confusion as formerly does. From the *New York Times*:

Ian Smart was formerly a member of the British diplomatic service from 1958 to 1969.

O. Edmund Clubb was former director of the State Department's Office of Chinese Affairs.

Leonard Katz, former reporter with the *New York Post* for more than twenty years, was named director of public relations for Monticello Raceway.*

Leon H. Keyserling was a former government economist.

Just how long, Mr. Keyserling, were you a former government economist?

Keyserling, who speaks English, is unable to reply.

I see. I submit, Mr. Keyserling, that the truth is that you have not at any time ceased to be a former government economist.

Keyserling consults his lawyer, but there is no way out. He agrees that he is still a former government economist and saves himself from a contempt of Congress charge.

It is possible that someone will be described as being presently a former government economist. The closest approach to this came during a baseball broadcast when Tony Kubek said that Brooks Robinson of the Baltimore Orioles had been voted the "greatest living third baseman of all time." Some insist that,

---

* Unfortunately for Katz, former reporter is a nonpaying job.

after a pause, Kubek or his partner, Curt Gowdy, added, "Currently." It is established as well as these things can be that during the same broadcast, Gowdy said of Tony Bartirome, trainer of the Pittsburgh Pirates, "He's the only trainer in baseball who used to be a former major leaguer." Presently.

Governor David Boren of Oklahoma is a man noted for what the NBC personnel department calls good oral and verbal communication skills. "My opponent," Boren once said orally and verbally, "already is setting the tone of his campaign to win the runoff. It is the tone of typical old politics—negative mudslinging." In contemporary America mudslinging is not enough. Negative mud must be slung. But then *war* is not enough. Admiral Elmo Zumwalt, retired chief of Naval Operations, has said that he is concerned about the possibility of another operative war in the Middle East. Zumwalt did not think it necessary to add that he preferred an inoperative war, or peace. Operative wars, after all, are full of—United Press International—fatal slayings, which are the worst kind.

Fatal slayings may be said to show human nature at its basest or, as the *San Francisco Sunday Examiner and Chronicle* has it, at its lowest nadir. Anyone in danger of becoming the victim of a fatal slaying faces, as former Secretary of Health, Education and Welfare Caspar Weinberger would put it, a major crisis problem. Particularly vulnerable would be, for the *Dallas Times Herald,* a recluse who likes living alone. Among the impressionable, such a problem may make the mind go, in Timestyle, entirely blank.

The mind that is entirely blank probably would not seem strange to State Senator Roscoe Dean of Georgia, who, when charged with cheating the state of $1424 in travel allowances, said that he was innocent and not guilty. It probably would not seem strange to Ron Nessen, President Ford's press secretary, who argued that published allegations that the CIA was giving money to noncommunist politicians in Italy "make it difficult to work with and continue to have a relationship with friends and allies around the world."

I had a theory—call it an imaginary fantasy—that it was not

the CIA but the CIAO, the dreaded Italian intelligence agency, that had been giving money to Italian noncommunist politicians. I did not pursue it, however, because doing so would have made it difficult for me to work with and have a relationship with Ron Nessen. There are some with whom I work with whom I do not have a relationship, but it tends to make everything take longer.

Others at the White House who worked with Nessen and either did or did not have a relationship with him announced in January of 1976 that President Ford would abide by the new election law totally and completely. That is abiding by the law on a scale scarcely comprehensible, except by the record company that put out a recording of *Così fan Tutte* that was totally complete.

The language in the White House announcement may have been Ford's. He has identified inflation as the universal enemy of 100 per cent of the people, and has described the country as currently facing three serious challenges, all at the same time. In his State of the Union message of January 1976, in which he proposed catastrophic health insurance for everybody covered by Medicare (when my time comes, count me out), he said that we could not realistically afford national health insurance, as though there were some other way to afford it. After losing to Ronald Reagan in the Texas primary, he promised to make a maximum effort in Indiana, and in the Alabama and Georgia primaries even more: a real sincere and very maximum effort.

Had James Schlesinger not been removed as Secretary of Defense, one might have guessed that he had been lending a hand in the press office, since Schlesinger had argued that reducing support costs made it possible to provide more combat capability and effectiveness. This was part of Schlesinger's plan for "turning fat into swords." It might have saved time and trouble to turn it into ploughshares.

Franklin D. Roosevelt, so A. Willis Robertson Professor of Economics at the University of Virginia Herbert Stein has pointed out in an article in the *Wall Street Journal,* holds the record for most times elected President in one lifetime. It is four. Should you want to ask Stein who holds the record for most times elected President in more than one lifetime (or less than one lifetime), you may of course try to reach him by telephone. I thought of it, but instead fancied that he was already engaged in a telephone conversation, talking with Henry R. Luce Professor of Urban Values at New York University Irving Kristol, and that there would be no point in my holding on. With those academic titles, such conversations take a long time:

"Is that Henry R. Luce Professor Kristol? It's A. Willis Robertson Professor Stein here. I'm curious to know, Henry R. Luce Professor Kristol, how you believe urban values are affected . . ." and off they go, the discussion culminating in a proposal by A. Willis Robertson Professor Stein, to which Henry R. Luce Professor Kristol agrees, that they broaden the scope of their inquiry and call Sebastian S. Kresge Professor of Marketing at the Harvard Business School Walter Salmon, Charles Edward Wilson Professor of Business Administration Emeritus at the same institution Robert W. Austin, Ralph Waldo Emerson Professor at the University of Massachusetts Adam Yarmolinsky, Norman Thomas Professor of Economics at the New School for Social Research Robert Heilbroner, Benjamin Franklin Professor of Economics at the Wharton School of the University of Pennsylvania Lawrence Klein, Edward R. Murrow Professor of Journalism at Columbia University Fred W. Friendly, Lawrence Wien Professor of Real Estate Law at the same institution Curtis J. Berger, and Marie Rankin Clarke Professor of Social Sciences at Claremont University Peter Drucker, and ask them what is happening to urban values in a changing world. William Edwards Huntington Professor of History and Social Science at Boston University Sam Bass Warner, Jr., could have told them. They're changing.

This does not get any questions answered about Roosevelt or about Presidents who had more or less than one lifetime, but such a disappointment ought to be taken in calm stride, as the Associated Press said the government of Laos was taking things. If it does make anybody calm but tense, as the *New York Times* found life in Beirut late in 1975, there is room for adjustment through the process the White House recommended for the Middle East, mutual compromise.

Someone in calm stride, so far as I can understand it, is strolling. For a horse, it is a canter. Somebody calm but tense might be trembling nonchalantly. As for mutual compromise, there is no other kind. This is true as well of mutual cooperation, which must be mutual if it is to be co. One-sided cooperation has been tried and found wanting, usually falling short by 50 per cent. An example of mutual cooperation is the Rose Bowl pact between the Big Ten and the Pacific-8 conference, which remains, the Tournament of Roses Association assures us, as firm "as the concrete in Pasadena's historic Rose Bowl stadium." The reasons? Two, says the Tournament of Roses Association—similar athletic philosophies and mutual cooperation.

Mutual cooperation requires a mutual agreement. The British, drawing on their long diplomatic experience, produced such a one with an announcement from Kensington Palace that "Her Royal Highness, the Princess Margaret, Countess of Snowdon, and the Earl of Snowdon have mutually agreed to live apart." Evidently it was a mutual agreement for a mutual separation. The British may want to take a phrase from American reporting of labor disputes: Both sides are far apart. When both sides *are* far apart, a man like President Ford's Secretary of Labor, William J. Usery, Jr., comes in handy. "Usery," an unidentified White House official told the *New York Times,* "is a tremendous guy to make peace on both sides of an issue."

Mutual cooperation must express itself in practical ways.* At the Rose Bowl, evidence of mutual cooperation may be seen in the fact that—a condition spotted by the *New York Times*—

---

* And not only in sports. Manhattan District Attorney Richard Kuh said, while describing a roundup of drug dealers, "All the agencies worked together cooperatively."

both teams are usually closely matched. It wouldn't be much of a game if only one were. It is best when they are coequal.

The concept of coequality is realized on the "Today" show, which has cohosts, though it does not bill coguests. I sometimes acted as cohost when Barbara Walters was the other cohost, but this can no longer happen because Miss Walters, in the summer of 1976, left her cohost copost at NBC to become a coanchor at ABC. It ended gracefully, at a farewell party, with cotoasts.

There were times when a cohost had little to do, partly because of the presence of the other cohost, and occasionally my mind turned to poetry, to Wordsworth and his cohost of golden daffodils. I also found myself thinking of the Atlantic Cohoast and the Pacific Cohoast, as well as the high cohost of living, and (this can become, as was said of the couple whose marriage failed, a bad cohabit), when in a religious mood, of the Lord God of Cohosts. Also of a burglar's associate interrupted in flagrante delicto: "Aha! Cohort in the act!"

The ideal cohost, had he not died before it could come about, would have been George M. Cohan, interviewing the Soviet Prime Minister, Alexei Kosygin, about peaceful coexistence.

In England, as we know, the rot has also set in. A broadcaster on the BBC has spoken of conspirators conspiring together, which suggests that opportunities exist for conspiring separately. It is painful to hear such things on the BBC, which can still, on occasion, speak with economy and directness. One such occasion came in July 1975, when John Stonehouse, a Labour member of Parliament, in prison and awaiting trial, did not eat. The BBC was frank enough to say that it did not know whether he had gone on a hunger strike or had simply lost his appetite.

Remnants of precise British usage survive. A man attempted to attack a notorious criminal with the intention of taking the law into his own hands. The police detained him, then sent him home with what was called appropriate advice. It may have been nothing more than, "I shouldn't do that if I were you, sir." British advice can be highly appropriate, and British ceremonial phrases poetic and succinct. When the House of Commons is to hold a debate in private, the signal is given by a member on the floor, who points to the galleries and says, "Mr. Speaker, I spy strangers." The Speaker then orders the galleries cleared, and the strangers, among them relatives and close friends, troop out.

The British don't always use understatement. At a meeting of shareholders of the British Leyland Motor Corporation, the chairman, Lord Stokes, explaining the disasters that had befallen the company, found his explanation being drowned out by slow clapping. Said Lord Stokes sarcastically, "Well, thank you for your support." Said one of the shareholders, "There is only one support you want because you are a bloody big rupture all the way through." It was a little too long to be ideal, but it undoubtedly enlivened the dialogue situation.

To call somebody a rupture is to speak metaphorically. The British do more of that than we do. The figure of speech is more comfortable for them because of the influence of the English poets and because, in politics, speech in the House of Commons is less declamatory and more spontaneous than speech in the United States Senate and House of Representatives. In Congress the seats face forward. In the House of Commons the government benches and the opposition benches face each other, and anyone who speaks does so with his supporters at his back or stands in their midst, with his adversaries glaring at him. It is an invitation to vivid speech. It is the atmosphere of the duel, the original eyeball-to-eyeball confrontation.

The Prime Minister may be facing the Leader of the Opposition across the floor fifteen or so feet away, with the one listening showing his disdain for what is being said by slumping down and putting his feet up against the table that stands below the Speaker's chair and separates the two front benches. Debate in the House of Commons is often a search for the phrase that stings the other side and delights your own, and the exchanges may be intensely personal. Aneurin Bevan of the Labour Party once pointed across at Winston Churchill and said, "When the Tories are finished with you, they will toss you aside as though you were a soiled glove."

Bevan may have remembered the occasion during the Second World War when Churchill called him "a squalid nuisance." The war years also produced one of Churchill's most scornful phrases, provoked by Mussolini's subservience to Hitler. Mussolini, Churchill said, was "the merest utensil of his master's whim." In any case, Bevan's remark also enlivened the dialogue situation.

Because of their literary tradition, and because so many British politicians have a university debating background, the House of Commons provides an almost universal welcome for a phrase well-turned. One was produced by a Labour member, Sidney Silverman, during a debate over the Middle East in the early 1950s. Ernest Bevin, who was the British Foreign Secretary, had for months been furious about the course events were taking. He felt that British policy was being excessively influenced by supporters of Israel, in both Britain and the United States. Bevin entered the House, spoke briefly and angrily, and left. Silverman rose to comment: "The right honorable gentleman," he said, "blows in, blows up and blows out."

It was a marvelous metaphor. How long Silverman had been nursing it, waiting for the propitious moment, I do not know. From the press gallery of the House of Representatives I heard one that I think could not have been nursed. It was the day that Grace Moore, the opera singer and moving picture actress, was killed in an airplane crash. When word of her death came in, Representative Jere Cooper of her home state of Tennessee asked for permission to address the House. "Mr. Speaker," he began, "a lovely flower has been crushed." Perfect.

The attempt to produce a metaphor sometimes produces a mixed metaphor, which resembles the redundancy. There is too much of it; it is overloaded; and it means that somebody is speaking who does not understand the terms he is using. Figures of speech can be treacherous; not everybody can handle them. And the mixed metaphor is a figure of speech that is out of control.

On the night of the 1976 North Carolina primary a guard at a textile plant in upstate New York heard a news broadcaster— it may have been a media analyst—say, "Reagan could use his victory in North Carolina as a springboard to rekindle his campaign." Throwing springboards on campaign fires was new to the guard, and he kindly wrote to tell me about it.

The most active metaphor mixers are politicians. For some reason—maybe they have to do more to be noticed there—this is especially the case in New York. John Lindsay, when mayor of New York City, presciently said, "It is necessary to lay the foundations for whatever difficult medicine the people will have to swallow." New Yorkers eventually swallowed much difficult medicine, and some of them thought that Lindsay himself was the chief ingredient. His search for other office failed, in keeping with the warning sticker pasted on some medicine bottles: CAUTION: Federal law prohibits transfer of this drug to any person other than the patient for whom it was prescribed. SHAKE WELL.

To Lindsay's successor New York's problems were identified flying objects in City Hall's superstructure. "These are not chickens just now come home to roost," said Mayor Abraham Beame. "They are birds of prey that have been with us for a long time, growing ever more assertive." Given New York's condition and a general disinclination to offend the birds of prey, which when not roosting were hovering unpleasantly in the city's air space, nobody seriously quarreled with Beame's analysis, though one citizen wrote a letter to a newspaper describing the city itself as an albatross bleeding rich and poor alike, which may have been what attracted the birds of prey. Beame's talent as a phrasemaker was overshadowed by the economic crises he had to grapple with. He refused to extend an official welcome to President Sadat of Egypt because, he said, Sadat supported a United Nations resolution that "seeks to revive a new form of racism." To revive something new is no mean trick.*

---

\* So is smelling out a mosaic. I wrote in *Strictly Speaking*: "Politicians should be encouraged to stand for what they believe in, not to try to smell out the exact mosaic of attitudes and positions that will appeal to the greatest number." How do you smell a mosaic? G. V. Underwood, Jr., of Hilton Head Island, South Carolina, wanted to know. It takes training.

New York politicians often think about what they, or their constituents, may be called upon to ingest. The Democratic leader in the state assembly, Albert Blumenthal, was enraged by a Republican charge that the Democrats had put the state in a pickle. "We find ourselves in this pickle," he replied, "because you bought that jar and filled it not with pickles but with water, and now you're trying to jam it in the public's face." The Republicans were so stunned by Blumenthal's accusation and a vision of themselves at factory gates as the early shifts arrive, shoving jars of water at workers who recoil and dash off to register as Democrats, that they did not reply, even to say something about a jar of another color. Another Democrat, Stanley Steingut, Speaker of the Assembly, would have known what to do with Blumenthal's jar. The easy thing would have been to carry it on both shoulders, but Steingut, to judge by his public pronouncements, would have put it on the back-room burner, where, from time to time, he likes to simmer legislative matters that he does not consider urgent. This kind of slow cooking goes on elsewhere. A survey on drug use in public schools which had been allowed to simmer in Seattle was said by an administrator, Dr. Robert Collins, to have "got kind of back-burnered because I didn't have time to pursue it in light of the upcoming levy."* Steingut, however, would not have found room for a bill that he thought would derail the ship of state, or which, in the words of Henry Wallace, would have sent the ship of state sailing down untrod paths. Steingut would rather have no legislative activity than that, even though he has recognized the danger of being buried by an avalanche of creeping paralysis.

Remarks of the kind Blumenthal made risk, in the *New York Times*'s flashing phrase, raking up old partisan wounds, which usually lie buried under the fallen leaves of yesteryear. The leaves, when blown away, reveal, etched in the sands of time, the question put by State Senator John R. Dunne of New York: "Who can predict what will remain after those winds of change have run their

---

* Also known as Up-and-Coming Levy, an uncommonly promising young politician of radiant personality.

course?" The winds of change, a relay team, took an early lead on an eight-lap track, with Tartan turf and banked at the curves, and then breezed home.

Old partisan wounds also exist outside New York, for example in Kentucky, where, in the 1975 primaries for governor, a Democrat, Todd Hallenbach, accused his opponent, Governor Julian Carroll, of "going around the state spreading mistruths and innuendoes. Julian Carroll," Hallenbach said, "has washed his hands on the courthouse steps of Kentucky communities like Pontius Pilate." He added, "The political machine has the gun on the people right now but the people pull the trigger and I think they'll pull it in the election booth." A correspondent in Henderson, Kentucky, pointed out to me that there is no Kentucky community named Pontius Pilate and denied that she intended to shoot herself while in the election booth. She thought it unnecessary to go that far to register a protest vote.

Washington produces metaphors that are mixed and mystifying. Senator Howard Baker of Tennessee said, when asked about the possibility of more hearings on Watergate, "The tip of the iceberg is the only thing showing. I'm not sure we can put it together." Representative Wayne Hays of Ohio, when he was chairman of the House Committee on Administration (administration is liable to broad construction on Capitol Hill), was pleased by a compromise on federal election legislation. "I think," said Hays, "this is a package that will fly." Air express.

Representative James Grover of New York put out a press release early in the Nixon Administration in which he announced: "The honeymoon is over between President Nixon and the Democratic-controlled Congress. The gloves are off and it's full speed ahead in attempts by the Democrats to impede the President's program." This means that the gloves must have been on during the honeymoon. It seems excessively formal.

Being around politicians in Washington affects reporters. Helen Thomas, UPI's White House correspondent, wrote this:

"Washington—President Ford said today America's economic

future looks brighter each day. But he accused Congress of drafting a federal spending blueprint that would ignite another inflationary cycle."

Two petitioners to the Federal Communications Commission got into the Washington spirit. They complained that there was not enough controversy on radio and television stations run by schools and colleges. "Educational broadcasters," they said, "should not draw the ivory towers about themselves as some sort of sacred cloak which permits them to choke off efforts for new, diverse, more broadly based groups to have access to radio and television permits." The ivory tower cloak that chokes has been approached only in the Puccini one-act opera *Il Tabarro,* in which choking takes place under both a cloak and cover of darkness. At the opera's climax the choker throws open his cloak and allows the lifeless body of the chokee to fall forward before the horrified eyes of the woman they both loved. This takes place on a barge on the Seine, and although there is no ivory tower, the Eiffel Tower glints metallically in the background.

The sacred cloak that chokes is a versatile weapon and would be more so if it had teeth. This may well be feasible, for there is a source of supply of teeth that legislatures are able to draw on at will. The source was drawn on when, as *Editor and Publisher* reported, sharp teeth were injected into the federal and Illinois fraudulent bidding and antitrust laws as a result of a reporter's brewing a scandal after six years of effort. What made the story news is that teeth go into brews—"Scale of dragon, tooth of wolf, Witch's mummy, maw and gulf Of the ravin'd salt-sea shark, Root of hemlock digg'd i' the dark"—more often than they come out of them.

Teeth are also injected into legislation under the parliamentary system, and the British are a step or two ahead of us here. They are specialists. The *Times* of London wrote: "We already have the machinery for the best sort of state intervention in the Design Council, which ought to be given not just pretty front teeth but molars, too, so it can be the catalyst in this now vital endeavor." A catalyst needs molars so that it can take the ferocious grip for which it is famous. Otherwise, public confidence, which has already taken a nose drop, will die by leaps and bounds.

The greatest metaphor mixer of our time, possibly of all time, is Representative Daniel Flood of Pennsylvania. He did not say, "At issue is a budding military program that six months ago in the first blush of prototype flying looked merely huge but now looms as the fighter plane plum of the century." The looming plum was developed, probably with the help of grafting techniques, by the *New York Times*. Flood did not say, "Angola Cements U.S.-Cuba Rift." The *St. Paul Sunday Pioneer* had the story on that, and aerial reconnaissance showed where the cement was being laid. He did not say, "Against every bone in my body, I'm sitting here twisting both arms." Representative Claude DeBruhl, of the North Carolina legislature, voting for a bill he opposed, tied up his arms that way, but the vote was by voice. Flood did not say that every child has his Achilles heel if only you can find the right niche in which to place him, or "That boy will be all right if we can get him to stop hiding behind his mother's apron strings." Years of research, observation, and practical work led social workers to those conclusions.

Flood did, however, tell a military commander that he was at the Rubicon and that if he did not change his ways he would be a dead duck. On another occasion, Flood questioned a Secretary of the Navy about some missiles. The missiles were, he said, pigeons that Congress had adopted a long time before. "When you get married that closely to something," he said, "you get very unhappy when it does not grow up to be an All-American. This thing is poohing out, and we do not like it." The witness objected only to "poohing out." This may have been out of forbearance, or because the Secretary was embarrassed about Congress's marrying pigeons that came under his jurisdiction and were not chosen as All-Americans.

Charles de Gaulle so angered Flood that Flood asked a Secretary of Defense during a closed hearing: "Do we have any alternative or are all our eggs in one basket if he picks up his marbles and goes home? Are we not in a badly exposed position? Are we not caught with our pants down out there?" The Secretary's reply was deleted from the transcript of the hearing for diplomatic reasons.

Flood's attention was attracted to Latin America by a proposal to build a successor to the Panama Canal. Speaking in the House, he said that a decision had already been made to build it in Panama. Proposals to build in Colombia, Nicaragua, and Mexico, he said, were merely straw projects in a fake horse race for propaganda purposes.

When I first called attention, years ago, to Flood's metaphor mixing, he wrote me that he had not been aware of it. "If I could mix a martini half as well," he added, "it would be a pistol, wouldn't it?" Flood has been a member of the House of Representatives for thirty years. What his life would be like if he left the House after all that time, I do not know. He might find himself, like a recent candidate for sheriff of Allen County, Indiana, sitting naked on the other side of the coin. It is cold on the other side of the coin, especially when the pendulum is swinging in the other direction, and those who find themselves there may want to get up off their hackles and leave, even if they have to cross a mesquite-infested prairie to do so.

The rest of us should help them, and if we really have our pulse on where people's heads are at, we will not be pettyune about it. Otherwise, we may find ourselves split right down to the grassroots.

# 8

# Myself Will Be Back
# After This Message

It was a day like most others. I had begun it by reading *In My Own Words,* by the gangster Mickey Cohen as told to John Peer Nugent. Why Cohen had to tell it to John Peer Nugent if they were his own words I could not figure out, but the book did live up to its advertisement, which said that it was bulging with profanity and malipropisms. Honi soit qui mal i prop.

Over lunch I learned, thanks to the London correspondent of the *Chicago Tribune,* that United States Ambassador Walter Annenberg had delayed retiring from his post for a week so as to attend the royal opening of Parliament, where his seniority admitted he and his wife to the front row, and with front row seats you could hardly blame they for waiting. The *Chicago Tribune* often sees through to the heart of things in that way. A *Tribune* columnist, Bob Wiedrich, has rebuked a court for failing to say that spanking a youngster today might save he or she from worse punishment tomorrow. Right as rain, I thought about lenient courts. Save we from they. Many parents depressed by their children's turning from the path of virtue may find mild corporate punishment to be the answer.

I read on and found the Huntington, New York, Pre-School suggesting to busy parents with a three- to five-year-old, "Why not drop he or she off at the school?" Why not indeed? With the start Huntington can give them, they may grow up to be as clever as Sonny Bono, whose business acumen, the New Haven, Connecticut, *Register* reported, helped land both he and Cher in relatively safe financial strata. This was considerate of Sonny because desperate strata were available at the time. Besides, she had left he.

Some men are confused about who did the leaving. They insert notices in newspapers that say, "Having left my bed and board, I will not be responsible for debts incurred or contracted by my wife." A notice of that kind often ends a relation that began with one more cheerful. Stouffer's Denver Inn posts a sign that greets newly married couples holding wedding parties there. I was lucky enough to see one:

> CONGRAD
> ULATIONS
> BRIAN & LIZ

I wondered whether this was a tradition begun by Congrad Hilton. It makes a good start down the road of life for those who have plighted their trough.

Speaking of weddings, here is a report on the youthful and immature marriage policies of the diocese of Springfield, Massachusetts, offered, with becoming modesty, by the diocese itself. Give the policies time.

I switched on the television set to watch the reflexive reflex, with Brent Musberger of CBS saying, "Phyllis, Irv, and myself will be back at half-time." Brent was followed by a commercial in which a man in a tavern was asked to choose between beers and announced, "I must say that the results were a surprise to myself and the others." Myself switched the set off and turned to a story by United Press International about a professor of psychology in

College Park, Maryland, who concluded that an attractive woman has a greater chance of receiving a light sentence if she has not used her beauty to perpetuate the crime. But would the sentence still be light if the woman's good looks illicited "oohs" and "aahs" in the courtroom? La donna e perpetuum mobile.

The *Telegraph-Herald* of Dubuque, Iowa, which was at hand, reported the King of Nepal coronated in a tradition-rich ritual. There is much we can and do learn from the East. Governor Edmund Brown, Jr., who is, one hears, a devotee of Zen, complained that before the 1976 convention many people had already coronated Jimmy Carter the Democratic candidate. That was done by Democratic party king makers meeting in a smoke-filled room and puffing on Corona Coronas before placing them on Carter's head.

*Time* magazine does not coronate. It decimates. It wrote, "China took another giant step toward consolidating the governmental and military leadership that was almost completely decimated by the Cultural Revolution and the struggle for power that followed it." To decimate means to reduce by a tenth. I interpret almost completely decimated to mean reduced by an eleventh. *Time* also wrote about an arrangement that "particularly rankles with younger Jesuits." The arrangement was outranked by older Jesuits. Rankle has its privileges.

There are many other wonders in the press, thanks in part to the dangling modifier. The columnists Evans and Novak report travel bills looking for votes—"As the favorite campaigner for conservative Republicans, Reagan's travel bills for himself and his large entourage consistently left his hosts bugeyed." The Associated Press finds annual profits that were somebody's sister and became the chairman of Dunhill's in London—"Since succeeding her brother as chairman in 1961, annual profits have risen from $1,300,000 to $14,000,000." United Press International alters the function of magnets—"President Ford keeps returning to Capitol Hill like a magnet." Or like a flame to the moth. Clive Barnes of the *New York Times* has a conversation with a mind of its own—"During the summer, walking through the ruins of Persepolis in Iran, my conversation with the guide turned to the theatre festival in nearby Shiraz." The *Times* also has a city taking extraordinary precautions—"As the plane nears Riyadh, the six-man security detail gets ready for landing. Unlike Damascus, they do not wear bulletproof vests on this stop." Damascus, jittery, never got off the plane. It couldn't get through the exit with the vest on.

I pressed on. AT&T is sending its shareholders a memorandom on "The Case for Congressional Action." If it catches on with the shareholders, AT&T may want to have it published commercially by Memorandom House. A Columbia Records press release declares Beethoven's late style perfectly congrous in its own terms and the distilation of a lifetime's experience in music.* Columbia offers recordings by the pianist Ruth Laredo of two works by Rachmaninoff, "Lilacs" and "Dasies." Giv me yur anser, do. The *Wall Street Journal* proposes a trial subscription at a savings of $3.50 over the newsstand price; I reject the offer, preferring a number of small saving. The *Judge,* published by the Syracuse University College of Law, reports that Dean Craig Christensen, questioned about the school's financial condition, responded, "While there are not enough funds to do what ought to be done, we're not in too bad of a position in the context of higher education in the seventies." If that is the dean speaking, or the paper, we are in very bad of a position in the context of higher education in the seventies.

Higher education goes on at Annapolis also. The director of candidate guidance, a Navy captain, has advised members of Congress of a meaningful service offered there through the Congressional Pre-Candidate Evaluation program. The captain wrote: "A candidate who receives an excellent or top candidate evaluation and is scholastically qualified, medically qualified and passed their physical aptitude examination will in all probability be offered an

---

* Johann Strauss's music was also perfectly congrous in its own terms. It was the congrous of Vienna.

appointment in the event they received an official nomination."
That seems only fair. If a candidate is passed their examination,
they should be nominated. Anchors ahoy.

The State Department has celebrated the Bicentennial by issuing special passports, with a deep blue cover and the Liberty
Bell printed in red, white, and blue on the pages, and bearing a
request to "all whom it may concern to permit the citizen of the
United States named herein to pass without delay or hinderance."
It is reassuring to see the State Department making that request.
Hindrance used to be hazardous enough. Nowadays hinderance is
the danger and can be disasterous. I have a Bicentennial passport,
and when it has expired I intend to keep it as a rememberance.

The Benton-Franklin Governmental Conference of Richland,
Washington, has announced that it is "accepting resume's in application for the position of secretary" and that "proficiency in typing, filing and standard office procedures are required." Benton
and Franklin want their money's worth. Ours is a mixed economy,
however, and private enterprise is giving government agencies stiff
competition in error making. The Stereo Festival of Great International Artists has advertised Lorin Hollander and the Tokyo String
Quartet playing Brahm's Piano Quintet in F-minor. A local shop
is offering reduced gown's on sale; another is selling groceri'es;
and John has chalked up on a convenient wall that he loves
Glady's. Hall Lebovitz, sports editor of the *Cleveland Plain Dealer,*
has written that the Cleveland Indians took a calculated risk by
hiring as manager Frank Robinson, "who's managing in Puerto
Rico must be regarded as inconsequential." The column was not
libelous, fortunately for Lebovit'z, who's paper might otherwise
have reported, as it sometimes does of others, that he had been
hailed into court.

All hale the *New York Times.* It reported the Greek community in Astoria, Queens, dancing to it's very own drummer. A
*Times* headline, "Mets Tour of Japan Will Cost About $2-Mil-
lion," worried baseball fans, but the tour was made by the Metropolitan Opera. The *Times* is in a class by it's self. I hate to be

finicky. I would rather, as the *New York Times* has put it, walk spritely on my way. Or read about the tennis-playing Evert sisters, Chris and Jeanne, both of whom, I was glad to see in the *Times,* are still close. How unfortunate if only one were.

So I read on in the *Times,* about the big oil spill that despoiled Portugal's coast, making off with a number of luxury hotels as booty; and about Yugoslavia's charging Croatians in exile with formenting terrorist acts, though surely that is a consequence Yugoslavia would expect in an atmosphere of intellectual fervent; and in the New Jersey *Sunday Record* about the policemen who waited until a suspect who had proceeded them to the door separated from his cainine friends, two Doberman pinchers. The suspect was arrested, but the police, who were not Doberman pinchers, let the dogs go. The *New York Times* tells me about the Italian financial institution known as the Bongo di Roma (its directors sit on the Bongo board), and about the 1000 per cent drop in the value of Chilean currency reported by C. L. Sulzberger. Before that I had thought that a currency could not lose more than 100 per cent of its value, but inflation in Latin America, as Sulzberger suggested, can be fierce. The Associated Press has the Watergate prosecutor attributing a nepharious plot to John Mitchell. There is no mention of the other dephendants. I come upon a story about Thomas D. O'Malley, state treasurer and insurance commissioner in Florida. "I'm not despaired in the least," said O'Malley. "In no way, shape or form do I intend to resign." Or as the *Miami Herald* put it in a headline:

> "I'm Not Despaired,"
> O'Malley Assures,
> Shuns Resignation

It was a great headline. It made me think of the proud boast by the *Birmingham News/Birmingham Post-Herald* on the cover of *Editor and Publisher:* No other media even comes close. A tenable claim. Other medias claiming to come close might fill a stadia, but Birmingham's medias are beyond their reach. So much for medias. As poor, bumbling, passionate, foolish, vengeful, tragic Canio the clown says in *I Pagliacci,* "La commedia e finita" (comedy is finite).

Claims to superiority are common. The restaurants that say that they are best might also fill a stadia, probably the Sugar Bowl, but the wise person has his own favorites. When my mind turns to food—an untoward development, since the legs usually go first, turning, in times of stress, to jelly—I think of smorgasborg, and then omelete assorti. I think next of an 8 per cent fillet mignion served in Amarillo, Texas—8 per cent is as much of that as I want to eat at a sitting; of Lindy's Crab and Seafood Market in Linden, New Jersey, which is open seven days a week and Sundays and holidays; of a restaurant in Buffalo, New York, that specializes in eye rib of beef, lean and succulant, cooked to your indiscriminant taste; and then of a stay at the Hollenden House, in Cleveland, where the restaurant listed appetite provacateurs, among them shrimp scampies, a mischievous but endearing crustacean. I long to go to a restaurant called La Diplemat, in Nashville, Tennessee, and I wonder what is on its menu. Perhaps Kitsch Lorraine, chicken en brochay, and two Irish dishes, O'Grattan potatoes and lemon moran pie.

A mad hunger takes possession of me and I am unindated by memories of the Granada Royale Hometel in Omaha, where a light and airy courtyard lends a sidewalk cafe affect to meals. I remember a roast beefe sandwich I had at the Red Lion Restaurant of the Beverly Hilton Hotel. Ah! Ye roast beefe of Olde England. Alors! Le petit strip sirloin at the Hyatt Regency Hotel at O'Hare Airport in Chicago, served with the Frenchman's favorite wine, Beaujolias. My minds skips to the Chez Bon Dining Lounge near L'Aéroport de Detroit; to the Board Room Restaurant in New York, which serves Les Asparagus de France, though not Les Tomatoes or La Lettuce; and to a plate du jour at a country club in North Carolina, where I saw a woman carrying a L'Tote cosmetics bag by Lancome. Her carriage suggested that her girdle was a Fleur d'Lace.

The French should be gratified that their cuisine is enjoyed across the United States. Stouffer's Denver Inn, where Brian and

Liz were congradulated, serves French Dip, consisting of sliced
Colorado beef on a roll with savory au jus so good it sets you humming. A cup of coffee, a sandwich and au jus. Au jus is turning
up in many places. I was offered a cup of it on an airplane. It appears to be a case of the wandering au jus. At Lake Tahoe, Shrimp
Provenciale is presented as evidence of one restaurant's Continen-
tal flare, and the DELInclineTESSEN restaurant features Escargot
Cognac and a galantina sandwich. I thought that anybody who
would drink Escargot Cognac must be galantina indeed, but a
preoccupation with food can lead you astray. When Mario Merola,
the Bronx District Attorney, made some comments about a super-
seder by Governor Hugh Carey, he proved to be talking about the
possibility that Carey would remove one prosecutor from office in
favor of another. I had assumed that the Governor was giving an
unusually large Passover feast for his Jewish friends. This seemed
not out of the question in New York politics.

My mind drifts back to the best, and only, baked lasange I've
ever had, in Hudson Falls, New York. It skips to a motel in Char-
lotte, North Carolina, where it was possible to begin a meal with
anti-pasto, a dish popular with those who dislike Italian cooking
(I am pro-pasto myself), and then, for those unable to make up
their minds about sauces, go on to Veal Parmigiana Milanese. All
roads lead to Rome, or elsewhere.

Mistakes enliven American life. Some, of course, are caused
by pomposity and make those responsible for them appear ludi-
crous. About others there is an innocence that it would be a shame
to lose.* In arguing for a civil tongue, I am arguing for naturalness,

---

* My mistakes in *Strictly Speaking* were caused by innocence. Joe
Ray, a copy editor on the Utica, New York, *Observer-Dispatch,* wrote:
"I was all set to credit you for clever work when I came across a real
blunder on page 139. You had Benjamin Franklin coming out of the
Constitutional Convention of 1776. It was the hot summer of 1787,
not 1776." When I put Campobello in Nova Scotia instead of New
Brunswick, a Canadian commented that geography was not my
province.

Another correspondent thought that religion was not my province even when it leads to mistakes. There is no reason that naturalness cannot be joined to correctness, but even when it isn't, clarity and genuineness can come together. More than this, we Americans don't have as much fun as we could with English. The fun is there to be had, but it requires some knowledge (which need not be formal), some imagination, and a sense of delight in what language can do.

I have been told that my view is cranky and pedantic, that I want to keep the language from growing and to impose a standard and rigid English on Americans. Far from it. Our language should be specific and concrete, personal, so that we don't all sound alike, eloquent when possible (for eloquence is hard to come by), and playful when possible (for wit is given to few). We spend much of our time speaking and writing. Must it be monotonous? One of the most cheerful pastimes is to play on words.

I was looking at an advertisement placed by the realty firm of Cleveland, Duble & Arnold, of Greenwich, Connecticut, for a waterfront estate with deep-water mooring, dock, float, and Har-Tru tennis court. An envious way of life, Cleveland, Duble & Arnold called it, and it seemed just right for me. My envy was insensate and knew no bounds. I had just picked up the phone to put in a bid for the estate when a man burst in.

"You are known to be arboring fugitives," he said in a gutteral voice.

I denied it.

---

either. The Rev. Ralph Kowalski, of the Church of St. Bede in Southfield, Michigan, wrote:

" 'Quo Vadis?' was not spoken by St. Peter but to him. It is reported, by usually reliable sources, that Christ, in a vision, confronted Peter when he was retreating from Rome to escape the persecutions. He asked, 'Quo Vadis?' whereupon Peter, in remorse, returned to his see and subsequent martyrdom."

I accepted the Reverend Kowalski's version rather than the rival version in which the question is put by Peter, because it seemed to me to offer a rare opportunity to use the word fraught. "Your book," I said to myself, "is fraught with error."

"Contain your indignance," he said. "There are radicals at large, flaunting the establishment."

I had read in Jack Anderson's column about the flaunting of the law by power-hungry men while they basked in the sunshine of Key Biscayne and San Clemente, and I thought the intruder's time would be better employed in going after them. I had even heard of cases of cavalier flaunting of the law. "Why come after me?" I asked. "Get the cavaliers."

He was not dissuaded. "In this very neighborhood," he said, "a man entered a woman's house with the intent of doing bodily harm to her person. She was in eminent danger. Luckily, the family dog, a laboratory retriever, who can be a holy terrier when aroused, arrived in the niche of time. I'm surprised that you don't know about it. You must be imperious to these things."

I said that I still did not know what he wanted.

"You have been surveilled," the intruder said. "We are well-vexed as to your activities."*

"Where did you get the information that led you to me?"

"It enamated from secret sources."

How would he describe the fugitives he was seeking? He replied that one of them had gray hair and an unrepossessing face, and was alienated with the government. She was wanted for smuggling and worked with a gang that specialized in falsifying ships' manifolds. She had been in a hospital, inflicted by monogram headaches, and while there had had a tubular litigation, which led to a blood clog in the lungs. They had had to stick a needle in her arm and feed her inconveniently. Nonetheless, she had recovered. An incredulous story.

I was moved to prayer and got out the fur skullcap I had bought in Peru, a llamalke. My visitor told me not to bother, it was all water over the wheel, and the point was that the unrepossessing

---

* A reader in Arlington, Virginia, told me that she does market research. In one study she asked people about their beer-drinking tastes and habits. The study was called "Beer Surveillance—Wave One." I suppose that the surveillers went ashore from the Potomac.

fugitive had been attended by a round-the-clock private nurse, and they could not understand how she got away.

I: A private nurse working round-the-clock may fall asleep.

He: I like a little repertoire as much as the next man, but these wisecracks only add more grist to the fires. Such half-hazard answers do not help to implant the goal of the investigation and risk rendering it mute. Your attitude is getting my dandruff up and becoming a craw in my throat.

I: There is no point in our hurling epitaphs at each other.

He: Can you vouch for the fugitive as a person of integrity and complete moral turpitude?

I: That puts me in a quondam, but in the transitory times we are passing through, I don't see how I can.

He: You are causing irreputable damage to my work, and you will have to bear the blunt of the punishment for it.

Could he not hold his judgment in obeyance? No, he replied; engaging in claudestrian activities was no joke. "I have deep-seeded emotions about this," he said, and he swept out into the bedrizzled streets in a high dungeon.

It occurred to me that the woman he was looking for might be Ma Gauche, a clumsy but well-loved gangster's moll from France. French gangsters rallied behind her shouting, "Dieu et Ma Gauche." I thought the investigator might be malingering outside, and when I opened the door I saw that he was in a large automobile. That clenched it. "Is this car public property?" I shouted.

"It is one of the prerequisites of office," he replied. "What's wrong with you? I crouched my request for information in polite terms, but you were on tenderhooks. You tried to pull a mirage over my eyes."

"That's a spacious argument," I came back. "You gave me a grueling."

He looked at me pityingly. "If you had helped me, you could have been capitulated into instant fame." Flush with victory, he drove off.

I was going out to buy some items at a shop called Sex Fifth Avenue. I turned on the radio to get the weather forecast and heard about a hurricane that was packing winds of up to eighty miles an hour. It was delayed until the packing was done. There was also financial news from India, where the Dhow-Jones industrials had fallen; news about China, for the Orient-oriented; proposals for a dental insurance plan that was opposed on the ground that it would cause wailing and nationalization of teeth; a story about a window dresser arrested while posing a serious threat; and another story about some people who behaved fecklessly and had not a single feck to their names, as a result of which the family fortune was placed in escarole.

Since the hurricane was still some distance away, I was preparing to leave when my visitor came in again.

"What is it this time?" I asked.

"Malocclusion," I thought I heard him say, and I asked whether the condition was giving him much trouble.

"It is not a condition," he said testily, "but an Irish tenor illegally in the country."

"How would anybody recognize him?"

"He cannot shape his vowels."

"But," I said, "that is an affliction so common it is known as the Broadway malady. Besides, he has cut only a narrow swathe in the world of music. Why not leave it to the police?"

"They are laxadaisacal about these things."

"It seems a waste of money to me."

My friend, as I had now begun to think of him, squared his jaw. "You'd better get a new prospective on things. A well-conceived expenditure, thanks to the cascade effect, will return the investment many times."

"Where did you learn that?"

"From the seventeenth-century financier Bernard Baroque."

"Cascade is le mot juste," I said admiringly.

He drew himself up. "Le Moe juste is a Jewish lawyer of French descent known everywhere for his sense of fair play."

I could see that he was becoming upset again, so I changed the subject. "I went to a recital last night by a secretary turned violinist."

"Who was it?"

"Yehudi Amanuensis."

I rubbed my eyes.

"What's the matter?" he asked.

"Conjunctivitis. I begin too many sentences with and."

"Have you heard about the French noblemen who all had the same name?"

"No."

"Pierres of the realm." This time he changed the subject. "What's your favorite restaurant?"

"It's an old-fashioned Russian one. I like to hear the instructions the proprietor gives the waiters."

"What are they?"

"See what the boyars in the backroom will have."

"You must excuse me," he said. "I'm off to dinner, to a small French restaurant I'm fond of. Le Premier Cri. Not pretentious, but it has won a cauldron bleu for its cooking. One dines there al fresno. I am especially fond of their canopies. It will be a sumptuary repast." He turned on his heel, his face betraying, I thought, a soupcan of sadness, and was gone.

"A richly redolent experience," I said to myself. "I must make a commitment of it to paper." And I did, though not before making out a check to the Washington Performing Arts Society so that it could, as it requested, list me as a benefictor. That is how I like to think of myself.

# Index